Passing the Superintendent
TExES
Exam

This book is respectfully dedicated to
Dr. Gary Cook
President
Dallas Baptist University
Dallas, Texas

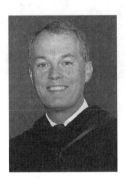

Dr. Gary Cook is one of the most genuine, sincere, and visionary
Christian leaders I have ever known.

At the time of this writing Dr. Cook, thankfully, is in remission from
acute leukemia. He has truly walked by the shadow of death and lived to tell about it.
He now continues to lead DBU in an exemplary Christlike manner.

We rejoice.

I ask all who read and benefit from this book to please pray for
Dr. Cook's continued good health, wisdom, family, and visionary
Christian leadership now and forever.
To whom much is given, much is expected.
With great respect and love,
Elaine L. Wilmore, PhD
November 2009

"For I know the plans I have for you," declares the Lord,
"Plans to prosper you and not to harm you, plans to give you hope and a future.
Then you will call upon me and come and pray to me, and I will listen to you.
You will seek me and find me when you seek me with all your heart."
(Jeremiah 29:11–12, New International Version)

Passing the Superintendent
TExES
Exam

Keys to Certification and District Leadership

Elaine L. Wilmore
Foreword by Jeanne M. Gerlach

CORWIN
A SAGE Company

For information:

Corwin
A SAGE Company
2455 Teller Road
Thousand Oaks, California 91320
(800) 233-9936
Fax: (800) 417-2466
www.corwinpress.com

SAGE India Pvt. Ltd.
B 1/I 1 Mohan Cooperative
    Industrial Area
Mathura Road, New Delhi 110 044
India

SAGE Ltd.
1 Oliver's Yard
55 City Road
London EC1Y 1SP
United Kingdom

SAGE Asia-Pacific Pte. Ltd.
33 Pekin Street #02-01
Far East Square
Singapore 048763

Printed in the United States of America

Library of Congress Cataloging-in-Publication Data

Passing the superintendent TExES exam: keys to certification and district leadership/Elaine L. Wilmore. Foreword by Jeanne M. Gerlach.
        p. cm.
Includes bibliographical references and index.
ISBN 978-1-4129-5619-2 (pbk.)

    1. School superintendents—Certification—United States. 2. School superintendents—United States—Examinations—Study guides. I. Wilmore, Elaine L. II. Title.

LB1768.P37 2010
371.2′012076—dc22   2009033586

This book is printed on acid-free paper.

09   10   11   12   13   10   9   8   7   6   5   4   3   2   1

Acquisitions Editor:	Hudson Perigo
Editorial Assistants:	Lesley K. Blake and Brett Ory
Production Editor:	Libby Larson
Copy Editor:	Claire Larson
Typesetter:	C&M Digitals (P) Ltd.
Proofreader:	Wendy Jo Dymond
Indexer:	Terri Corry
Cover Designer:	Michael Dubowe

Contents

SECTION III: THE REAL DEAL: PRACTICAL APPLICATION

SECTION IV: AFTER YOU PASS THE TEST

Foreword

*P*assing the Superintendent TExES Exam: Keys to Certification and District Leadership is a must-read for those who are preparing for the superintendent TExES exam and school district leadership. Elaine Wilmore provides readers with relevant discussions about and explanations of key information that will help them improve their test performance and ultimately their lifelong leadership skills.

Elaine is one of the few experts we have today who is effective in combining theoretical and practical information in a way that helps readers make important connections between what they know and how they apply that knowledge to everyday issues. Not only is she an expert in the field, she is also a role model who has enjoyed continued success in helping future K–12 leaders achieve success. Once again, she shares her expertise with us. I am honored to find in her a colleague who is helping to create confident, well-informed leaders.

Jeanne M. Gerlach, Dean
College of Education
The University of Texas at Arlington

Preface

*P*assing the Superintendent's TExES Exam: Keys to Certification and District Leadership has been written in the same voice and format as the highly successful *Passing the Principal TExES Exam: Keys to Certification and School Leadership,* also by Elaine L. Wilmore. As students who had previously not been successful read *Passing the Principal TExES Exam,* they have spoken with one voice in praise of the book that actually helped them pass the test. In many instances, they had been unsuccessful multiple times. Finally, they tried *Passing the Principal TExES Exam,* found it to make sense of the domains and competencies for them, and then went on to pass the test!

Due to this success there have been many, many requests for this follow-up book, *Passing the Superintendent TExES Exam: Keys to Certification and District Leadership.* Readers of the first book will feel immediately comfortable with this new book, as it continues in the same manner of explaining the competencies in realistic terms anyone can understand. The author welcomes school and district leaders "home" to this new book and reminds them that she still likes Hershey's chocolate and pink roses when they pass the top TExES exam in the State of Texas. (Some things never change.) Dr. Wilmore also hosts multiple administrator TExES preparation seminars across the state annually. For more information on those classes, see www.elainewilmore.com.

Acknowledgments

As always, I must acknowledge and thank my family and closest friends for putting up with me while I stressed over getting this book written. Thank you to my outstanding husband, Greg, who always helps me with the graphics and who also coordinates all my TExES preparation seminars. On top of that, he still loves me after 36 years of marriage, which really is a pretty remarkable thing. I love you too, honey! Much love also goes to our son and daughter, Brandon Greggory Wilmore and Brooke Elaine Wilmore, for encouraging and supporting all my dreams. Particular kudos this year go to our middle daughter, Brittani Leigh Wilmore Rollen and her husband, Ryan Rollen, for presenting us with our beautiful and brilliant first grandchild, Blair Elaine. It is definitely true that there are few joys as pure and wonderful as that of a grandparent's love. We love you, Blair Bear! You are our beautiful and brilliant baby girl!!!

I continue to be blessed beyond reason with friends I love, respect, and trust. With arms open wide, I applaud them for putting up with me. These include Helen and Wes Nelson; Kathy and Dr. Joe Martin; JoNell and Larry Jones; Renea, Emily, and Dr. Wade Smith; Becky and Dr. Bob Shaw; Dr. Linda and Ron Townzen; Dr. Mary Lynn Crow; Bob and Sallie Feavel; and lifelong friends Melda Cole Ward and Kerry Van Doren Pedigo. A particular huge thank-you to Becky and Bob Shaw for again allowing me the wonderful opportunity of rest, solitude, quiet, and renewal for my soul while writing much of this book at their lovely home in Winter Park, Colorado, my favorite place on earth. I start smiling when we get into town and don't stop till we leave. All are *great*.

I must also thank Kee Badders, Gail Peace, and Marsha Bridges for their outstanding technological and editorial assistance. Wow. You are amazing, and I thank each of you with all my heart.

To all the great folks at Corwin, particularly Executive Editor Hudson Perigo, her able assistants, Lesley Blake and Jingle Vea, and former Corwin executives Robb Clouse and Douglas Rife, what can I say? Thank you for believing in me way back in the beginning. You are the best.

Last, I thank my parents, the late Lee and Irene Litchfield, to whom I owe all that I am or ever will be. They taught me values and to care for others plus they always supported my lifelong love of reading, libraries, and all things book related. I miss you both so much. We will be together again someday . . . in Heaven.

Love always,

Elaine

About the Author

**Elaine L. Wilmore,** PhD, is a professor and the chair of Educational Leadership, Counseling, and Foundations at the University of Texas of the Permian Basin. She has previously served at Dallas Baptist University as assistant vice president for educational networking and program director for the MEd and EdD degrees in educational leadership. She has formerly served as special assistant to the Dean for NCATE accreditation, chair and associate professor of educational leadership and policy studies at the University of Texas at Arlington (UTA), president of the National Council of Professors of Educational Administration, president of the Texas Council of Professors of Educational Administration, and president of the board of trustees of the Cleburne Independent School District, where she served for nine years. She is the founding director of the Dallas Baptist University EdD in educational leadership and multiple programs at the University of Texas at Arlington including all initial programs, educational leadership, and the Scholars of Practice Program. While at UTA, she was also principal investigator for multiple grants for innovative field-based principal preparation programs. She has served as director of university program development at UTA, where she also developed and was the original chair of the faculty governance committee for the College of Education.

Dr. Wilmore is professionally active and has served on many local, state, and national boards. These include having served on the executive committee of the National Council of Professors of Educational Administration, the American Educational Research Association Executive Committee on the Teaching in Educational Administration SIG, the Texas Principals Leadership Initiative, the Texas Consortium of Colleges of Teacher Education; she has served as a program/folio reviewer for the Educational Leadership Constituent Council. She holds the unique distinction of being one of the few to have served as both a private and public school district board of trustees member.

Dr. Wilmore was a public school teacher, counselor, and elementary and middle school principal before she moved to higher education. In addition to her significant work in educational leadership, assessment, and program development, she enjoys reading, writing, walking, traveling, music, and spending time with those she loves. She is the wife of Greg Wilmore; the only child of her late beloved parents, Lee and Irene Litchfield; the mother of three wonderful children, Brandon Greggory Wilmore, Brooke Elaine Wilmore, and Brittani Leigh Wilmore Rollen; and a fabulous son-in-law, Ryan Rollen. A top highlight of her life is her first grandchild, Miss Blair Elaine Rollen. Elaine has four outstanding Pug dogs named Annabella Rose, Isabella Lace, Tug the Pug, and Zoe' Eloise that she loves to cuddle with. In her limited spare time, she dreams of learning to play the violin, viola, and cello and of taking leisurely hot, peach bubble baths by candlelight in Italy.

SECTION I

The Knowledge and Theoretical Base

Welcome To Our World!

Many of you have read and used my *Passing the Principal TExES Exam: Keys to Certification and School Leadership.* Since its initial publication, people have so graciously said how much they liked it, how it made the competencies seem so real, and how it helped them pass the Principal (68) TExES exam. Some people said that they had been unsuccessful in passing the test until they read my book.

All of this has warmed my heart. I like it when my books or classes help people. I like hearing from them afterwards and knowing I have made a difference in their lives in a small way. We desperately need more principals whose hearts are committed to helping teachers teach and students learn, to improving society through their relationships with students, families, and the community, and who have heeded my call to make the world a better place, "one student and school at a time" (Wilmore, 2003).

Soon after *Passing the Principal TExES Exam: Keys to Certification and School Leadership* was released, students, universities, and Regional Education Service Centers began to ask when I was going to write a superintendent's TExES preparation manual. Surely, with the dramatic shortage of superintendents as well as principals, a book to expand and explain the superintendent domains and competencies was also needed. In response to that demand, today you are beginning to read *Passing the Superintendent TExES Exam: Keys to Certification and District Leadership.* To those of you who are familiar with the first book, this one will read and feel like a homecoming. It will use the same format, and of course, it will still utilize the same "voice" of teaching by using real-life examples as the first book. Although there are ten superintendent competencies, whereas there were only nine for the principal exam, you will still see a lot of similarities in concepts. All of the same knowledge and skills that you have successfully applied for campus leadership are also essential in district leadership. Just as you have previously transitioned from "thinking" like a classroom teacher to a principal, again, you will now learn to think more globally. What is best for the entire district rather than just one campus? How can you lead for improvement of the entire district, to establish a true learning community, and to make strong data-driven decisions rather than what is politically expedient? How can you enhance your moral core to stand tall ethically and withstand the external pressures that fall on all superintendents? These are the things we will be discussing in *Passing the Superintendent TExES Exam: Keys to Certification and District Leadership.*

To those of you who are not familiar with my principal TExES preparation book or who are from out of state, let me explain what the test and its background are all about. In the state of Texas, as in many other states, there is a rigorous examination that potential educators must pass before becoming eligible for certification. In Texas, this test is called the TExES (Texas Examinations of Educator Standards) exam. We have a TExES exam for everything from initial teacher certification to the superintendency. There is tremendous pressure on candidates to pass this test. Without it, no one can become certified. There is also tremendous pressure on preparation programs for their students to do well. Potential test takers from both inside and outside the state are looking for tools to help them achieve their goals of getting certified and becoming a world-changing Texas superintendent.

Universities and alternative preparation programs are working hard to address both the knowledge and philosophical base upon which the TExES exams are formed. The superintendent (064) exam is built upon a framework of ten competencies within three domains. We are fortunate in Texas that our competencies are directly aligned with the national Educational Leadership Constituent Council (ELCC) standards. This alignment is shown in Figure 1.1.

It is assumed that test takers have received knowledge and research preparation through their educational providers. This book will supply needed supplemental resources for the knowledge base, but it is not intended to substitute for a master's degree or advanced certification program. It will focus, however, on the philosophy necessary to *think* like a learner-centered superintendent. There is a deficit in candidates making the transition from *thinking* like a principal to *thinking, reflecting, reacting, and responding* like a superintendent. All of the knowledge in the world is useless if a test taker

Figure 1.1 Alignment of Educational Leadership Constitutent Council (ELCC) Standards With TExEX Domains and Competencies

	ELCC Standard 1	ELCC Standard 2	ELCC Standard 3	ELCC Standard 4	ELCC Standard 5	ELCC Standard 6	ELCC Standard 7
TExES 001					√+		√
TExES 002	√+						√
TExES 003				√+			√
TExES 004						√+	√
TExES 005		√+					√
TExES 006		√+					√
TExES 007		√+					√
TExES 008			√			√	√
TExES 009			√+				√
TExES 010	√			√			√

√+ = Primary Focus of Standard   √ = Addressed in Standard

5

cannot *think* in the way the test was developed. *Passing the Superintendent TExES Examination: Keys to Certification and District Leadership* addresses the philosophy as well as the skills superintendents must have within each of the three domains and ten competencies. This book provides test-taking tips for before, during, and after the exam. Specific attention is given to in-state and out-of-state test takers. Each competency, 001 through 010, has its own chapter that explains the competency in detail with examples. The end of the book concludes with additional resources that will be helpful to candidates as they develop their knowledge and philosophical base necessary to pass the test and pursue careers as lifelong leaders of learners.

As with all my books, this one is written in an informal voice. There are real-life stories and applications integrated into each competency to help you connect abstract concepts to today's reality. It is absolutely necessary that you learn how to integrate your knowledge and skills into application for success both on the test and as a world-changing superintendent. My goal is for *Passing the Superintendent TExES Examination: Keys to Certification and District Leadership* to be helpful and friendly. It was not designed to be stuffy or aloof, but to actually help you understand exactly what the competencies mean and how to apply them on the TExES exam and in real life.

THE DOMAINS

The superintendent TExES examination is divided into three domains with ten competencies. The domains are as follows:

- Leadership of the Educational Community
- Instructional Leadership
- Administrative Leadership

There are four competencies within Leadership of the Educational Community, three within Instructional Leadership, and three also in Administrative Leadership. Questions on the test are designed to address specific competencies. However, they are not evenly divided. Approximately 40% of the questions will address competencies within Leadership of the Educational Community. Approximately 30% will address different competencies from Instructional Leadership. The final 30% will focus on Administrative Leadership. There are no absolute numbers of questions per competency or domain. My goal is for *all* of you to get *all* answers to the questions correct regardless of which domain or competency they come from. However, a student does *not* have to score 100% to pass the test. For many students, just realizing they do not have to make a *perfect* score on the test helps take the pressure off. This is a good thing because half the battle of passing this test is a mind game. In other words, psychologically you must know you *can and will succeed.* It is my intention for all of you to win the mind game. You should walk into the testing center *cool, calm, collected, confident, and almost downright cocky.* This mental attitude is necessary to keep your stress level down. When your stress level goes up, your productivity goes down. I don't want that to happen to you. As shown in Figure 1.2, I want your stress level down and your productivity way up. Therefore, you should be cool, calm, collected, confident, and almost downright cocky as you prepare for the test, so you will be prepared to conduct yourself likewise during the test. Practice now for what you are going to do then.

Many people put great emphasis into trying to figure out exactly which competency each question addresses. Although we will discuss this strategy, it will not receive undue attention. Remember, if our goal is to get *every* question correct, why do we care which competency the question came from? We do not. We want to get *all* the questions right. However, upon becoming thoroughly familiar with each of the competencies, as you will in Chapters 3 through 12, you will recognize key words and concepts that will guide your selection of the appropriate answers to get *all* the questions right . . . or at least enough to pass.

In addition, there is significant overlap of key themes within the competencies. Since the test is largely a timed mind game, why would you want to stress yourself out with the clock ticking, worrying if a question is addressing competency 001 or 003? Who cares? The important thing is to understand, integrate, and *live* the competencies. Make them your Superintendent's Bible. Beginning this minute, let your walk match your talk in modeling these competencies in your daily life. Then on the day of the test, walk in there and ace the TExES exam because you are already living the philosophy upon which it is built.

Figure 1.2 Anxiety and Productivity

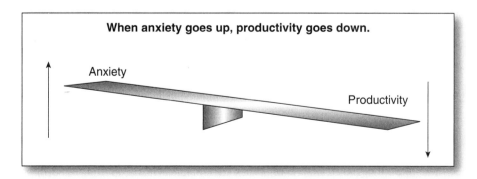

If you think there was a lot going on as you serve or served as a principal, you haven't seen anything yet. Think of leading a school district as orchestrating a really good jazz band. As the musicians practice before a performance, they individually sound like a whole lot of *noise.* Everyone is doing his or her own thing, warming up, and getting ready for the concert or gig. But once it gets going, everything comes together. The musicians play as a team. They are great musicians who have worked hard, who have practiced together, and who have the common goal of producing really awesome music. Because they have done those things, the concert begins and their *practiced skills* turn into a true art form as they blend together, bending and flowing with the ebb, the crescendos and decrescendos, the tempo, and the dynamics of the music to produce something truly beautiful.

There has been no greater time than now that our school districts need great leadership. We need you to lead the jazz band, to bring all the different parts of the system together into one melodious whole. We do not want or need noise such as when we were practicing to get where we are. We need *jazz.* We need to knock the world dead through the integration of the ten competencies and skills we will be studying together here. Today's society needs and deserves superintendents who can direct districts like smooth jazz bands. As long as people in the district are doing their own things, independent of each other, all we will get is noise. I would think we could all agree that we have had enough noise coming out of our schools. Now it is time for jazz, and you are the one leading the band. We want, we need, and we will have beautiful music. You will be a great superintendent. You will be a learner-centered leader with passion, vision, and purpose who will lead the district to win a Grammy, or at least be at the top of the list of successful districts regarding No Child Left Behind (NCLB). Every district deserves to be a part of a learning team. All children deserve to be a part of a district that is focused on success for every facet of their lives. Every child, every teacher, every support staff member, every administrator deserves to be a winner.

For too many students today, there is little hope for the future. I want *you* to be the best leader any district (jazz band) ever had. *You* will be the leader that does what is right instead of what is easy or bureaucratic. *You* will be the superintendent that facilitates your district and community in developing a common vision and a solid purpose built on identified common shared goals and values. *You* will be the one to change the world . . . or at least your district. *You* will become an *awesome superintendent,* or I will come back and haunt you.

But, first you must pass this test. Are you ready to get started?

GETTING STARTED

Section II of this book includes Chapters 3–12. Chapter 2, It's All Good, will give you the global view of how you will achieve your goal of passing the test. This test is merely a gatekeeper designed to see that you have a specific learner-centered philosophy of district leadership as portrayed in the domains and competencies. It portrays *entry-level* administrative skills and expectations. It is a passable test. You *will* pass this test. There is absolutely no reason for you not to, because, after all, you are studying from *my* book. I teach leadership and research at the University of Texas of the Permian Basin. I also teach TExES preparation classes all over the state. It brings me great joy when students from any of them contact me to let me know they passed the test. I get really excited! After all, that means there is one more human out there ready to join my journey, my quest, my passion toward improving the world. In the rare instance someone is unsuccessful in a testing attempt, it grieves my heart. It makes me sad and that is *not* a pretty sight. I feel sure that you would much rather make me, and yourself, very, very happy. So follow the directions I provide for you in this book. Even if they don't make sense to you, do them. They have worked for zillions of people before you, and they will work for you. To borrow from the fine folks at Nike, *Just do it!*

In *Passing the Principal TExES Exam: Keys to Certification and School Leadership,* I encouraged people to let me know when they passed the test. I also told them that I have a strong preference for *pink* roses and chocolate. My favorites are Blue Bell ice cream, of course, and Hershey bars, plain with no nuts. There are already enough nuts in education. We do not need any more. They seem to propagate just fine on their own without our help.

Through the years, you would be amazed how many Hershey bars and roses I have received. Sometimes a student will send one Hershey. Others have sent nine, one for each of the nine competencies they passed on the Principal TExES exam. And, believe it or not, I do get roses. I love me some pink roses! In fact, roses have followed me across the state. This spring, after a wonderful five years at Dallas Baptist University, I moved to the University of Texas of the Permian Basin. When I got back from spring break, I had a dozen roses waiting for me in the certification office. All of the staff was waiting for me to get there to see whom the roses were from. They had thought I had a secret admirer. I did! It was another wonderful person who I did not even know but who has read my book and passed the Principal TExES exam.

Now, folks, I am not telling you that you must send me Hershey bars or roses when (not if) you pass this test. You truly do not have to. But it can't hurt. . . .

Chapters 3–12 provide detailed attention to each of the ten learner-centered competencies. If you have never even *heard* of them up to this point, that is all right. By the time I get through with you, you will be *living and breathing* them. You are going to know those competencies inside out. You will be reciting them to your families and friends. If you do not have a family or friends, I strongly suggest finding some. They will be a great support system for you to celebrate with *when you pass the test!*

The next component, Section III, addresses the integration and application of all you have learned in Section II. You will become skilled at how to analyze data, learn specific test-taking strategies, and create your very own personal success plan as you prepare for the test and afterwards. Last, in Section IV, we will discuss the final logistical tasks you need to do to actually become certified as a superintendent in the Great State of Texas. We will then tie it all together in Chapter 16, That's What I'm Talking About. By the time you walk in to take your TExES exam, you will be so prepared that all you will want to do is go in there and pass it so you can go forward to improve the world and eat more chocolate. This test is just a headache to get in your way. So let's get rid of this headache by *passing the test the first time!* Why bother having to take it again? Are you ready? Let's go!

It's All Good

GLOBAL OVERVIEW OF THE THREE
TExES SUPERINTENDENT DOMAINS

It is critically important that you understand the theoretical framework, or philosophy, upon which this TExES examination is built. It is explained via the three domains and ten competencies we will study in the upcoming chapters. If you do not truly understand what these mean and how to apply them for district improvement, you will not pass this test. Therefore, it is imperative that you take great measures to analyze what each of them means and to brainstorm examples of ways you could utilize them as a highly effective superintendent. Figure 2.1 demonstrates for you the connections and linkages from the theoretical framework to the domains and competencies to passing this test and, finally, to improved district leadership.

As introduced in Chapter 1, the ten competencies are placed into three domains:

- Leadership of the Educational Community,
- Instructional Leadership, and
- Administrative Leadership.

There is significant overlap in the integration of the individual competencies because the superintendency is not a segmented, compartmentalized job. Daily roles and tasks *do* overlap. As they are busy fighting the fires of a normal district day, the average superintendent does not stop and ask, "Gcc, I wonder if I should respond through Competency 002 or 006?" That is why it is important for you to know the competencies inside and

Figure 2.1   Steps to Success

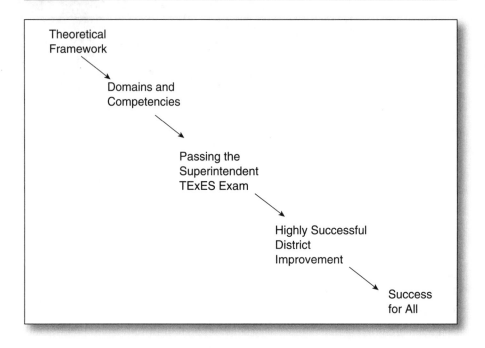

out, to internalize their concepts, so you can respond reflectively and instinctively. Before getting into the detailed analysis of the competencies within Chapters 3 through12, let's talk about several specific formatting components of this book as well as the theoretical framework of the three domains.

Key Concepts

I will provide you with three key concepts for each of the three domains to help you identify them and keep them straight as you are preparing for the test and afterward as you grow and learn as a superintendent. These key concepts will capture the basic essence of what that domain is about. They will help you focus as you dig deeper into each of the competencies. During the test, these concepts will serve as clues to help with the identification of the right answers.

Important Recurring Themes and Concepts

It can be overwhelming to look at the entire SBEC Superintendent TExES Preparation Manual and see all those pages of domains, competencies, and practice decision sets. However, it is not nearly as daunting as it may seem. The test developers actually have some favorite concepts and use them over and over. They simply spin them different directions within each of the three domains.

Think of it this way. If a new set of parents name their baby "Sherry" and "Sherry" is not a family name, we can assume they must like the name Sherry. The same is true with this TExES exam. There are themes and concepts that the domains and competencies use over and over. We will call them our Sherrys. Just as new parents must like a name or they would not have picked it, the same will be true for us. Once we identify the Sherrys when you see them in answer options, realize they are there for a reason. The test developers like them. They are the test Sherrys. Pick and use them accordingly. A sampling of Sherrys appear in Figure 2.2, Important Recurring Themes and Concepts: The "Sherry" List. Watch for the Sherrys in Chapters 3 through 12, see if you can identify more, and be particularly vigilant to watch for them as you take the actual examination.

Figure 2.2   Important Recurring Themes and Concepts: The "Sherry" List

- All
- Alignment
- Collaborate
- Data-Based Decisions
- The 1–2–3–4 Plan
- Develop—Create—Design
- Articulate—Communicate—Market
- Implement—Put Into Action
- Evaluate—Assess
- Culture
- Climate
- Vision
- Lifelong Learning
- Professional Development
- Enhancing Everything: How Can I Make It Better?
- Ongoing, Continuous Assessment
- Multiple and Diverse Forms of Assessment and Measurement
- High Expectations
- Facilitate
- Student Advocate
- Student Needs
- Participatory Leadership and Management

"GUESS MY FAVORITES"

Each competency chapter (Chapters 3–12) will feature my personal favorites of the activities or "bullets" provided by the State for each competency. While anticipating ahead of time which ones they will be, you will be internalizing the thought process of the test as well as synthesizing what the concepts actually mean. Therefore, it is not that you really care which of the bullets my favorites are. It is simply a strategy to help you internalize the philosophy of the test, a skill necessary for success. For example, say that during the test you have eliminated two of the four choices. But you cannot decide between the remaining choices which one is correct.

By practicing the "Guess My Favorites" technique presented here, you will actually be practicing thinking like I am thinking. On normal days, you may not care what I am thinking. But on the day of the test, you do care very much. So if you cannot decide between two or more remaining answers, ask yourself, "What would Elaine put? Which one would be her favorite?" Then go with your gut and mark what your instincts tell you. For the purposes of passing this test, you will have practiced guessing my favorites ahead of time so that you can guess them again during the test. *That's why* you care what my favorites are. It is to help you pick the right response when you are downright stumped.

During the discussion of the domains in this chapter, I will tell you which is my favorite as a preview to the actual competencies to be presented in Chapters 3 through 12. However, in those actual chapters, I will *not* tell you my favorites until *after* the discussion. The purpose is to get you to think and be able to predict which ones are my favorites as *practice for the test.* Consider it a game. See if you can figure out which my favorites are before I tell you which ones they are. If you can, you are off to a great start in that competency. You will also be on your way to becoming a wonderful learner-centered superintendent.

THE IDEAL SUPERINTENDENT

For just a few minutes, stop and close your eyes. Visualize in your mind an ideal superintendent that you know or have worked with. If you cannot think of an ideal superintendent, make one up.

Perhaps your person will be a combination of the skills or talents of several different superintendents that you know or wish you knew. Think about all this real or imaginary person does or could do. What makes that person great? What attributes or characteristics does the person have? What makes this person better than the average superintendent? What makes this superintendent outstanding? Take a few minutes to really think about this. *Do not blow this exercise off!* It may sound too simple to be important, but it is going to help you build your personal ideal theoretical framework for the test and for your entire career as a superintendent.

After you have given this due diligence in serious thought, open your eyes. On a piece of paper, write the adjectives or other words you used to describe this Ideal Superintendent in your mind. Take several minutes to do this. At first, obvious characteristics will come to your mind. Write them down.

Then when you think you have thought of all of the characteristics, dig a little deeper. Come up with some more. It is in this deep *reflection* that you will get to the real depth of being an ideal superintendent. List fifteen to twenty-five good characteristics. Do not give me that look of incredulousness. You can do it! Dig deep and come up with some more really good ones. Write them down.

If possible, prepare for the test with a friend. Study and discuss this book together. Do this exercise together. Then compare your results. Your results will be multiplied as you collaborate. You already know how you think. By the time you finish this book, you will definitely know what I think. Get inside the mind of your friend in this exercise to expand your way of thinking. In so doing, you will likely have identified several common characteristics. That is fine. Great superintendents *do* have many things in common. However, you and your friend may also have come up with some *different* characteristics. Are they things you can agree upon? Are they things you both agree constitute this new mega Ideal Superintendent? Develop a master list of characteristics of your Ideal Superintendent. Discuss them together. *Keep this composite list to review periodically before the test.* Why did you select these traits and not others? Elaborate on your thought process. This is what becoming a *reflective* practitioner is all about. Again, this exercise is worth true effort. It will help you clearly define the Ideal Superintendent in your mind so that you will recognize these traits and characteristics when you are selecting correct responses on the test.

Once you have developed your Ideal Superintendent, think about that superintendent and *no other* for the rest of your life. Think about that person as you study the domains and competencies. Think about the Ideal Superintendent as you are selecting responses to the practice "decision set" questions you will find at the end of this book. Above all, think *only* about the Ideal Superintendent on the day you take your TExES exam. Do *not* think, "That response is not reasonable," or "That response is not practical." Forget reasonable and practical! Think *ideal!* You can be reasonable and practical when you are picking out a new car. On test day, think *Ideal Superintendent!* Think, "Dr. Wilmore says 'Forget reasonable and practical. Think ideal!'" Pretend I am a little bird sitting on your shoulder chirping, "Ideal! Ideal! Ideal!" at you the entire time you are testing. There are enough reasonable and practical superintendents out there that have totally lost sight of the district vision. Think *ideal* to change the world . . . one student, campus, and district at a time. Besides, I will hunt you down and haunt you if you ever turn into a bureaucrat. So let's just not go there. It won't be pretty. How many bureaucrats do you know that are true visionary idealists? Not many and certainly not you. You will be a student-centered superintendent who always chooses to do what is right rather than what is easy.

PRETEND

Remember when you were a child and played pretend games? It was fun to pretend to be an astronaut or president of the United States. (Time has not run out. . . .) Well, let's play the pretend game again. Let's say that you are not into this whole Ideal Superintendent concept. Let's say that thinking "ideal" is just too far-fetched for you, and you think it would never work in the real world. Let's say that you cannot think of a single good reason to hold the Ideal Superintendent up as a standard for choosing TExES exam responses.

Pretend. Just pretend that you actually believe you can become an Ideal Superintendent and really impact your district, town, and world. Feel how you would feel if that was really true. Savor that good feeling as it seeps through you, and work toward it forever.

There is no law in this world that says you have to believe in any of the traits of the Ideal Superintendent. Maybe your goal in life *is* to be a bureaucrat. If that is true, I have two things to say to you:

1. On the day of the test, *pretend you believe like crazy!* You may not buy the philosophy of the Ideal Superintendent, but I can guarantee you one thing. The developers of this test do, and right now, they hold all the cards. Therefore, if you want to pass this test, pretend like crazy that you are the Ideal Superintendent and make answer selections accordingly.

2. What if you cannot do it? You just cannot do it. You do not buy one word of this whole Ideal Superintendent concept. You really *do* want to become a bureaucrat. You have wanted to be a bureaucrat all your life. Your mother raised you to be a bureaucrat, and you are looking forward to it very much. You have a burning desire to sit in the superintendent's office listening to Mozart, doing as little as possible, and never, ever actually becoming invested in the lives of others. In fact, the whole thought grosses you out. You want to be left alone in the sanctity of your office to do . . . virtually nothing. However, you would like to look really important while you do it.

   Here is what you do. Put away this book. It will not do anything for you except raise your blood pressure since there is absolutely nothing in it designed to develop your bureaucratic skills. You can quit your job. You do not need to be a superintendent after all. In fact, you do not even need to be in education. Go look for another job where your attitude will not impact society. Take up golf or knitting. Cook spaghetti. But the last thing you need to be doing is holding back the forward movement of changing the world through improved and democratic districts. You, after all, were born to become a bureaucrat. We do not need any more bureaucrats in our districts. We have plenty. We need educational improvement specialists who are focused on enhancing teaching and learning.

Now that you have learned the way you are supposed to *think* to pass this test, and you have learned to *pretend* on test day and to guess my favorites, let's get started with those wonderful three domains.

THE THREE DOMAINS

Domain I: Leadership of the Educational Community

Key Concepts: Culture, Climate, and Vision

Domain I is *Leadership of the Educational Community.* Approximately 40% of the test is from this domain. I love this domain. It is my personal favorite. It likely will not take you long to figure out why.

In a nutshell, Leadership of the Educational Community concentrates on all the things a superintendent should do to develop and nurture the culture, climate, and vision of a school that is *supportive* of all stakeholders and that helps them succeed. Who is a stakeholder? Everyone. Absolutely no one is left out. The term *stakeholders* goes hand in hand with other key TExES terms and concepts, which are the *learning community* and *school community*. The idea is to get everyone possible involved, especially the board of trustees, in identifying common values, developing a shared purpose and vision of the district, and developing goals and strategies to achieve them. The school community consists of teachers, counselors, paraprofessionals, auxiliary personnel, parents, community members, businesses, churches, and *everyone else* interested in the district and student performance. The more people you can get involved, the better. People support what they help build. Our districts and campuses need all the help and support they can get.

You may ask, "What if my district is downright awful and under review by the Texas Education Agency (TEA) at this very minute? What if it is located in a part of Texas that isn't exactly what you had in mind? The idea of getting parents or anyone else involved is pretty far-fetched." Fine. Think far-fetched. Remember, we are focused on the Ideal Superintendent. The Ideal Superintendent learned at the feet of Winston Churchill. During the bleakest moments of World War II, Churchill was known for telling the people of England that they would never, never, never give up. The English never did give up. Eventually, the Allies won the war, preserving freedom and democracy for the next generation. It did not happen by anyone taking the easy road or rolling over and playing dead. It came through hard work, perseverance, and collaboration with other countries.

The same is true within Domain I. The Ideal Superintendent will never give up. It does not matter how bleak the circumstances, Ideal Superintendents pick themselves up, dust themselves off, and start all over again. It takes intense resiliency to be a great school superintendent. Anyone can be a lackluster, status quo superintendent. Who on earth needs more of those? Certainly not us! We are Domain I superintendents, intent on facilitating everyone collaborating for a better tomorrow. It *is* a vision thing. Never give up. Never.

Can you see why this domain is my favorite?

Domain II: Instructional Leadership

Key Concepts: Curriculum, Instruction, Staff Development

Domain II is the "meat and potatoes" of the superintendency. It is what makes us different from CEOs or managers of any other organization. We are here to lead *school districts,* not shoe stores. What are we selling? Curriculum and instruction. How do we do that? Through improved staff development. Notice, I did not say "teacher" development. That would be limiting. We do not want to limit anything or anyone. Les Brown says to reach for the moon. Even if you do not reach it, you will land among the stars. Awesome superintendents want to nurture and develop everyone. They reach for the moon and only settle for the stars if they have to. However, landing among the stars sure beats having a district that TEA and the NCLB folks think is downright awful.

Always dream big. I tell all my students that if they do not remember one single other thing that I teach them, please remember to dream big dreams. I even have it programmed in my university voice mail message and e-mail signature. You would be surprised how many people leave messages commenting about what a surprise it is to hear anyone encouraging them to "dream big." I always wonder, isn't dreaming big what schools and universities are for?

Is that not what *any* school district is for? Domain II is all about improving curriculum and instruction for the benefit of *all* students. It is about finding ways to nurture and develop staff so they can be the arms, legs, and voices of improved curriculum and instruction, to meet the developmental and learning needs of *all* students.

Not that we are excited about it, but now would be a good time to introduce TAKS. For you out-of-state folks, TAKS is the Texas Assessment of

Knowledge and Skills. It is a *really* big test in Texas. Students begin taking it in the third grade. They keep taking it until they pass the high school exit version. If students do not pass the high school TAKS, they do not graduate, period. It does not matter if they make straight As. It does not matter how many honors or advanced placement classes they have taken. It does not matter if they have a wonderful scholarship waiting for them. They must pass that test. Students who fail TAKS in the early grades are identified as "at risk." Plans are made to remediate them so they will pass the following year, to help get them on track for the high school exam. The public schools of Texas are under intense pressure for students to do well on TAKS. The state accountability system is directly linked to student success or failure on TAKS. TAKS, or its former version, called TAAS (Texas Assessment of Academic Skills), is referred to in the TExES examination. For our testing purposes, respond to them as if they were the same thing. It is not the purpose of this book to address whether TAKS, or TAAS, is a good thing or a bad thing. It does not matter. It is the law. If it is the law, then it is the hand we are dealt. If it is the game we are playing, you can guess what we must do. *Win!*

If we think of TAKS as a game that we intend to win, we must become coaches and produce a game plan and strategies to make sure that we do. How many coaches do you know who say, "Well, guys, it's Friday night in Texas. Half the town will be out there waiting to see you play. They do not really care if you win or lose. They just want to see you looking good in those great uniforms. It warms their souls." In *Texas?* I do *not* think so. In Texas, teams are expected to *win.* If they do not win, serious things can happen. It is downright un-Texan not to win . . . or not to die trying.

Domain II is about winning. Think "curriculum, instruction, and staff development." They are our tools for winning. They are our game plan. They are the "meat and potatoes" of who we are, and why we are here. To create a better world, we must have an educated society. Meat and potatoes. Curriculum, instruction, and staff development. Domain II. Think big, dream big, plan hard, and win.

Domain III: Administrative Leadership

Key Concepts: Resources, Facilities, and Safety

The third domain, Administrative Leadership, is different from the first two. Domain I deals with the culture, climate, and vision of the district. Domain II deals with the "meat and potatoes," the staples of teaching and learning, which are curriculum, instruction, and staff development. But Domain III goes in a slightly different direction. It deals with the *business* of running a district. It is absolutely necessary that superintendents are committed and passionate about the district vision and that they do everything possible to augment appropriate curriculum and instruction. Yet, even with all that, if the superintendent cannot appropriately *manage* the daily operations of the school, that person will not be ultimately successful. As in the classic Broadway musical, *The Music Man,* there will be trouble in River City.

Domain III deals with budget, resource allocation, financial management, personnel management, facilities, and safety. For a superintendent to be effective, that person must provide a *balance* of leadership and management skills. It will not matter if you are passionate about meeting the needs of all students if you cannot plan for and allocate funds properly. Your school board will not be *at all* pleased if you run the district into a deficit. If you do not "get your act together" financially, they will see to it that you do not have that problem anymore because you will no longer be the superintendent. That will not help the cause of proactive superintendents who really want to make the world a better place through increased literacy, problem solving, and critical thinking skills, so Domain III is very, very important.

There is one specific aspect of Domain III that bears emphasis here as well as within subsequent chapters. That is the issue of school safety. We used to think of student protection as having a safe facility, with access for persons with disabilities, or having secure playgrounds or having the right number of fire, tornado, or other emergency drills. Unfortunately, our world has changed with needs far beyond that. With school shootings like Columbine in Colorado and church shootings like Wedgwood in Fort Worth, violence has infiltrated the two most sacred institutions in America: our places of worship and our places where we educate our young. This is wrong. It is *very* wrong. There is no way to justify it.

But it is also reality. To ignore that these things are occurring would be to hide our heads in the sand. Positive, proactive, energized superintendents never hide their heads in the sand. They are always looking forward by having emergency plans in place and practiced for any situation imaginable. Further, in their proactivity, they are also trying to be constantly vigilant, watching for signs of students, staff, community members, or others in need and *meeting* those needs so there will be *no* need to put emergency plans into place.

In the spring of 2001, Santana High School in California experienced school violence at its worst. Just a few weeks later, another high school in the same district was also hit by violence. At the time, news reporters interviewed school officials. The officials said they had a plan for violence intervention. Teachers, students, police, and everyone else involved worked the plan. They did everything they were supposed to do. They were lucky. Everything worked and no one was harmed. What concerned the superintendent though was what *triggered the need* to put the plan into action. That is the hard part.

Identifying and meeting the needs of everyone is an overwhelming and some-times daunting task. But the Ideal Superintendent is the one taking this test, and Ideal Superintendents are never exhausted or daunted. They never wear out or become stressed. They are the Superintendent Energizer Bunnies who keep going and going and going and going.

The Ideal Superintendent never quits going. The Ideal Superintendent works constantly, without letting up, to maintain a safe and effective learning environment for *all* students. Anything less than this 100% focus is just going through the motions and is not ideal.

You have now been introduced to the global view of the three learner-centered domains. The next ten chapters delve into the specificity of the ten competencies that fall within them. From the beginning, you will know that if a competency (or a test question) has something to do with vision, climate, or culture, it is likely a Domain I question. You should look for a test response that also directly relates to the same issue. The same is true for the other two domains. Remember your key concepts to help you keep your domains straight.

Remember also that sometimes the test will give you excellent answer choices . . . that do not answer *this question.* Underline important words in the prompt and question to keep yourself focused on exactly what is being asked. If they give you a wonderful selection choice, but it does not answer the question and is not in line with the appropriate domain, forget it. It may be beautiful, but it is not the right answer for *this question.* If the question has to do with developing a district budget and one of the answer choices is, "Thomas Jefferson was president of the United States," that may be true. But it does not answer this question. Do not let them trip you up with answers that are true, but do not answer the question. Be very cautious about this because it is one of the main ways of distracting you from the correct response. We are delighted that Thomas Jefferson was president of the United States. But it does not help us pass this test. Now let's take a look at those ten competencies so we can knock the top out of this test. Even Thomas Jefferson would be proud of you.

SECTION II

The Theoretical Framework

Learner-Centered Values and Ethics of Leadership

DOMAIN I: Leadership of the Educational Community

DOMAIN KEY CONCEPTS: District Culture, Climate, and Vision

COMPETENCY 001:

> *"The superintendent knows how to act with integrity, fairness, and in an ethical manner in order to promote the success of all students."*

It is interesting that this "ethics" competency is 001 for superintendents, yet a very similarly worded competency for principals is 003. Perhaps this is pure coincidence. Or perhaps it indicates the top priority that superintendents should place on acting with "integrity, fairness, and in an ethical manner" to help insure the success of all students.

THE SUPERINTENDENT KNOWS HOW TO . . .

- *Serve as an advocate for all children.*

There are people who do not understand why special programs—English language literacy, extra- and cocurricular, transportation, and multiple other programs—even need to exist. It is the role of all educators, and particularly superintendents as role models, to articulate the importance of a free and appropriate education for every child. Some programs, policies, and rules exist due to federal and state legal issues and regulations. Others exist to enhance district programming by district choice. But all programs exist to improve the educational opportunities for every student in the district regardless of whether English is their first language, whether they do not have a stable home life (which, consequently, can cause multiple problems both at school and in society), whether they are involved with drugs, whether they are not totally positive where their next meal is coming from, or whether they appear to simply not understand or care about their own education. The superintendent must lead the way in stressing the importance of meeting the needs of every student for the short- and long-term benefit of society.

- *Model and promote the highest standard of conduct, ethical principles, and integrity in decision making, actions, and behaviors.*

Ethics and integrity are displayed in the way you conduct yourself personally and professionally. Actions speak louder than words. Regardless of what kind of lip service is paid to a mantra of all students being able to learn, talk is nothing unless you put what you say into practice on a consistent and daily basis. Trust is so easy to destroy, and equally difficult to regain. It is important to listen to your constituents with a truly open mind rather than to make decisions based upon preconceived perceptions. Decisions should be data driven rather than perception driven. It is very hard to repair the damage and credibility among district staff if they think you have made a decision based on bias, partiality, or just plain stubbornness. Constituents need to know and understand why decisions are made. As often as reasonably possible, they should be made collaboratively. People will support what they have helped to develop or decide. Before taking actions, ask yourself if it will pass the "smell test." If someone else sees you doing something that you think is perfectly fine, would it "smell" to them? Would it cause suspicion? Would they think you are getting by with doing something they cannot, or should not, do? If so, this action smells. Remember, something can be totally innocent, but given just the right twist, it can appear unethical. Be cautious. Always act with discretion. Err on the side of caution. Someone is always watching and listening and, often, more than likely to repeat what they saw or heard freely . . . and with that dangerous little twist. The concept of modeling and promoting "the highest standard of conduct, ethical principles, and integrity in decision making, actions, and behaviors" may sound like common sense. Unfortunately, too often there is an uncommon lack of common sense. Be careful. Be prudent. As shown in Figure 3.1, always measure everything you do by your moral compass. You have one. Use it.

Figure 3.1	Highly Effective Superintendents Have a Moral Compass

- Act With Integrity
- Act Fairly
- Act Ethically

- *Implement policies and procedures that promote district personnel compliance with the Code of Ethics and Standard Practices for Texas Educators.*

The *Code of Ethics and Standard Practices for Texas Educators* has recently been revised. It is available for free at http://info.sos.state.tx.us/pls/pub/readtac$ext.TacPage?sl=R&app=9&p_dir=&p_rloc=&p_tloc=&p_ploc=&pg=1&p_tac=&ti=19&pt=7&ch=247&rl=2 (retrieved January 19, 2009).

Read it and really think about what it says. There is nothing there to shock you, but it is a good, solid review for this competency. The test will not ask you to quote it. However, it will expect you to know what it says, be able to live by it, to model it for others, and to encourage your staff to do likewise. The test will not come directly at you with questions that shout, "Are you ethical?" Rather, your interpretation of ethical behavior will be embedded in the answer choices. Therefore, be on full alert to make sure you select the most ethical response.

- *Apply knowledge of ethical issues affecting education.*

In today's world, the only constant is change. It seems it is becoming a regular occurrence to see or hear in the news that some educator has behaved in an unprofessional, unseemly, or downright illegal manner in relation to a student. This is particularly horrifying in regard to sexual harassment issues for both sexes. Therefore, it is of utmost importance for superintendents to stay abreast of and be able to apply things learned from current events and legislation in regard to ethical and legal issues involving students, personnel, and the community. You must be the stalwart of ethical behavior in the way you conduct your own life both professionally and personally. Any of these issues could lead to your demise as well as presenting a bad perception for the district. Keep everything you and the system do aboveboard. Do not just assume ethical- and compliance-related issues will take care of themselves. Research what district policies and procedures are in place to ensure they occur. If none exist, make it a priority to see to it that they are developed, articulated, and implemented to ensure the district is in full compliance with the *Code of Ethics and Standard Practices for Texas Educators* as well as all federal, state, and local policies and regulations.

- *Apply laws, policies, and procedures in a fair and reasonable manner.*

Be consistent. Even if you think there are circumstances where a law, policy, or procedure is cumbersome or irrelevant, as long as it is in place, you must use it. Nothing will get a superintendent in trouble, inside or outside the district, more than the perception that various people or groups are treated differently from any others. You must be extra careful about this in relation to any family members or friends who are employed by the district. It doesn't take much to give some negative community members something to exaggerate, misrepresent, and spread around. The more a story gets told, the worse it can become. By the time it gets back to you, it could be so distorted you barely even recognize it. Remember, there are people who live by the mantra of "Do not mess up my misperceptions with your facts. I like it in my mixed-up world. I get attention by passing around wrong information. It makes my day." The solution is to proactively avoid giving anyone anything at all to talk about. You do this by applying all laws, policies, and procedures in a fair and reasonable manner and doing so in a manner that is above reproach.

- *Interact with district staff and students in a professional manner.*

Be friendly. Be visible and interactive on campuses, in the community, and in professional organizations. Be impartial and treat everyone with both respect and dignity. Some community members may be crazy, and everyone might know it. Treat them respectfully anyway, even if you are privately biting your tongue. You are the first face and voice of the school district. It is your job to set the district culture and climate of professionalism to all people at all times and in all circumstances, even when they are crazy.

GUESS MY FAVORITES

My favorites in this competency should come as absolutely no surprise. If it isn't the role of superintendents to do these things, then whose is it?

- Serve as an advocate for all children
- Model and promote the highest standard of conduct, ethical principles, and integrity in decision making, actions, and behaviors

IMPORTANT POINTS TO REMEMBER

- Does this action pass the "smell" test?
- Is this action, decision, or attitude in the best interest of students or just easiest for the district to implement?
- How will others view this decision? Is it totally ethical?
- What leadership characteristics will others see in me by the actions, decisions, and attitudes I display?
- Was this an open-minded, data-driven, ethical decision, action, or attitude?

Learner-Centered Leadership and District Culture

DOMAIN I: Leadership of the Educational Community

DOMAIN KEY CONCEPTS: District Culture, Climate, and Vision

COMPETENCY 002:

> *"The superintendent knows how to shape district culture by facilitating the development, articulation, implementation, and stewardship of a vision of learning that is shared and supported by the educational community."*

A case could easily be made that 002 is the most important competency of them all. If you understand and are able to apply it, almost everything in the other nine competencies will fall under this umbrella. This competency is all about the district vision. Everything we do, say, or research should be something that is going to facilitate reaching the district vision. Therefore, it is of utmost importance that the entire school community work together to determine exactly what the district vision is or should be, what the things are that will be needed to achieve it, and how it will be articulated, measured, and, if necessary, modified. The district vision should briefly summarize everything the district hopes graduates will know, be able to do, and exemplify. It includes the knowledge base, skills, and attitudes every graduate will have. It is the master plan into which campus and departmental plans feed. All together, every district campus, department, and function should have its own vision, its own goals, and its own strategies for attainment, measurement, and, if necessary, revision. Obtaining the vision is what everything we do every day is all about. If, based upon a needs assessment and an audit of how time in classrooms is actually being spent, it is determined that things are occurring that do not support the vision, they are a waste of time and should be eliminated. The vision is the single most important element that the superintendent should lead the district, both macroscopically and microscopically, into developing, articulating, and using. It is the purpose for which the district exists. Figure 4.1 shows highly successful superintendents must be true visionaries.

Figure 4.1	Highly Successful Superintendents Are Visionaries

- Develop a District Vision
- Articulate the District Vision
- Implement the District Vision
- Good Stewardship and Evaluation of the District Vision

Photo courtesy of Sharon Ni Wang and Shota Teruya

What is your district vision? What steps are being taken to achieve it, if any? If the answers to these questions do not come immediately to your mind, you have serious work ahead. Without a clearly articulated vision, the district is approaching education by a shotgun approach, where pellets/actions are flying everywhere, instead of a rifle approach, where the bullet is clearly focused upon a specific target. It is time we as districts start working smarter rather than harder. The district vision is the tool by which this can occur.

This competency is so important that before we get into the examples of superintendent performance, I want to walk you through it virtually word by word. There is so much packed into this short sentence that I am afraid you will miss something if I don't make sure you get it piece by piece, bit by bit.

The competency begins with, "The superintendents know how to *shape* district culture . . ." It does not say the superintendent comes in and immediately tells everyone what the culture will be, how it will be developed or nourished, or even how it will be measured. It says the superintendent shapes the district culture. This is important because of what the verb *shape* says. It is not autocratic. It is collaborative with the interest and input of the entire district community being highly involved in its development, articulation, and implementation. So watch for questions about the vision, or anything else that has answers that come from an autocratic, top-down perspective. They would be wrong answers. Watch for answers that show the superintendent as shaping what is going on. Those are the correct answers.

The superintendent's primary role is to be a *facilitator.* It is not your job to do everything. That's what you have other people for. However, it is your job to facilitate that everything gets done. Therefore, when you are shaping everything from the vision to learner-centered objectives or bond elections, you are leading as a facilitator. From the perspective of this test, that is a good thing. You are not heavy-handed. You are not a dictator. You are a facilitator, working with the input of virtually everyone to reach collaborative decisions together. Thus, you are shaping the district culture rather than defining it exclusively from your own perceptions and views. Thus, you are a superintendent who "knows how to shape district culture by *facilitating . . . ,*" in truth, virtually everything.

Now let's talk about what I call the 1–2–3–4 Plan shown in Figure 4.2.

Figure 4.2 The 1–2–3–4 Plan

1. Develop—Create—Design—Plan

2. Articulate—Communicate—Market

3. Implement—To Put the Design Into Action

4. Steward (Nurture, Sustain) or Evaluate—Measure—Assess

Go back to the competency itself. Take your pencil and mark 1 by *development,* put 2 by *articulation,* 3 by *implementation,* and 4 by *stewardship of a vision of learning.* As shown in Figure 4.1, we are numbering them 1–2–3–4 because that is the order they are given to us. Why is that such a big deal?

There are several reasons. Throughout the test, there will be multiple times when you are asked which of the following things the superintendent would do "first" or "initially." While all of the items may look good, before answering, go back to your 1–2–3–4 Plan. Ask yourself, which one of these things goes with number 1, which is *developing?* What other words could they possibly use that are synonyms for *developing?* Make yourself a list right now so that when you see any of those words on the test, you will recognize them as meaning the same thing as *developing*. Some choices include the following:

- Planning
- Designing
- Creating
- Building
- Expanding
- Growing

It is important to utilize good planning first, because we do not want to put the cart in front of the ox. For example, a good contractor does not simply start building a school without first studying the previously developed architectural designs to know how the school is supposed to look when it is finished. The *details* of the construction have already been worked out as part of this planning process. Stephen Covey (1990) tells us to begin with the end in mind. That's what we are doing when we work collaboratively with others. We accomplish this developmental planning process first through developing or enhancing a district culture in Domain I, by improving and aligning the curriculum with developmentally appropriate instructional techniques in Domain II, and by facilitating a district budget based on student needs in Domain III. It makes no difference what the issue, domain, or competency is. First, or initially, important collaborative planning must take place. We do not reach conclusions by "seat of the pants" techniques or make long-term decisions by what is most popular at the moment. Instead, good superintendents involve others, research and analyze data, and subsequently develop plans for the issue based on accurate information rather than perception. That is why the first element in the 1–2–3–4 Plan is so important and why I am putting such attention on it right here in the beginning. Remember it throughout all ten competencies.

The next element in the 1–2–3–4 Plan is *articulation*. To articulate something means to communicate whatever it is in a way that other people can understand. This goes beyond being a language issue even though that is certainly extremely important. As educators we have a tendency to talk in our own jargon (some people call it "educationese") that noneducators cannot comprehend. Anything we say to the community, to teachers, to parents, to whomever must be done in a way that they clearly understand and are able to comprehend. They may not agree with us, but at least they understand what it is we are trying to get across and the rational upon which it is based. Therefore, whether we are articulating the district culture in Domain I, new curriculum or teacher assessment in Domain II, or a crisis management plan in Domain III, it is important that it is done in a way that people can understand. Remember, you cannot clearly articulate something until after it is developed. That is why *articulation* is number 2, whereas *development* is number 1.

Take a minute to brainstorm other words that the test developers could use in questions instead of the word *articulate*, but which mean the same thing. This is important because it is likely what they will do. Some words they may use are the following:

- Communicate
- Explain
- Elaborate
- Define
- Discuss
- Market

The exact word they use is not the issue. It is the *concept* of making sure you understand it is our job to clearly communicate everything that is going on in the district to all stakeholders. People cannot support what they do not know or understand.

The next step in the 1–2–3–4 Plan is *implementation*. We cannot implement, or put into place, anything *appropriately* unless it has been properly developed and communicated to all stakeholders. Therefore, to maximize our district productivity, before putting any new program in action, or after working to improve an existing function, we first put great effort into developing it properly by using current research and data and then ensuring that all stakeholders know what we are doing, how it was developed, why it is important, how it will be assessed, and what their roles are. After *all* of that has been done, we actually implement whatever it is we have been working toward. It is important that we keep all of these things in the right order. Do not skip steps. If, in an effort to save time, we skimp on any step, or simply skip it, the results will manifest themselves in the lack of *maximized* success in the implementation. In today's districts, we do not have time for anything less than *maximized* success, so do not skip or skimp on steps in the 1–2–3–4 Plan. You will reap what you sow.

Think about other words or phrases that the test developers could use instead of implementation. Some could include the following:

- Strategies
- Techniques
- Action plans
- Putting something in place
- Starting a new program or curriculum
- Enhancing an existing program or curriculum
- Just doing it

The last element in the 1–2–3–4 Plan is *stewardship of a vision of learning*. Everything we do should be assessed. A retired Navy admiral once said, "What gets measured gets done." But the *stewardship* of the vision goes beyond assessment and measurement to the nurturing, sustaining, enrichment, and refinement of whatever it is we have been working so hard on in steps 1, 2, and 3. This is the building up of our people when they are tired. It is the lifting up and encouragement of teachers and support personnel as they are pressured and stressed beyond all measure at state testing times. It is being the district shepherd who takes care, nurtures, and sustains everyone toward their roles in the development, articulation, implementation, and refinement of the vision. It is a very important component because it pulls the first three together. It is also the one that is least likely to actually take place in a consistent, systems-approach manner. We need to take care of each other. If we do not take care of our principals and teachers, they can eventually become so tired, so "soul fatigued" (Wilmore, 2007) that they can no longer come close to working at peak performance.

Being an educator is a calling. Being a superintendent is a special calling. Superintendents are more than business managers (Domain III) or instructional specialists (Domain II). Superintendents are the role models of professionalism in creating a district culture that values a collaboratively developed vision. Figure 4.3 shows the distinction between reality

Figure 4.3	District Improvement Process, Moving From Reality to the District Vision

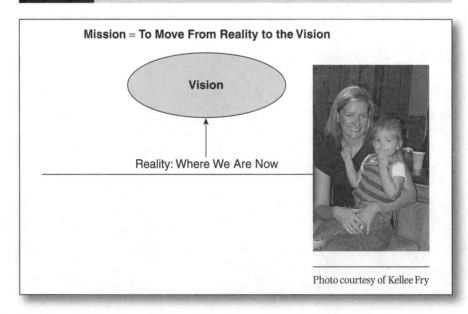

Mission = To Move From Reality to the Vision

Vision

Reality: Where We Are Now

Photo courtesy of Kellee Fry

(where we are now) and the district vision (where we want to be). Our mission, thus, is to move us from reality to the vision. Saying this may sound easy. Accomplishing it is definitely not.

This "vision of learning "will be "shared and supported by the educational community" when it is developed with everyone working together toward a common goal of success for every student regardless of who they are, what their race, religion, gender, mobility, financial status, or demographics are. Unfortunately not everyone agrees on everything all the time. Figure 4.4 illustrates that all people do not hold the same views and belief systems. Our goal is to seek, find, and utilize even the smallest area of common ground as a starting point for creating the district vision and everything else.

| **Figure 4.4** | Identifying and Respecting the Common Ground |

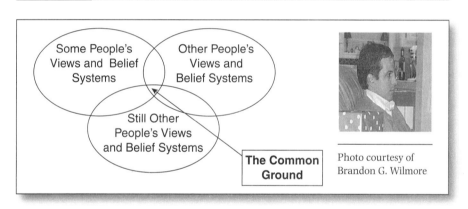

Some People's Views and Belief Systems

Other People's Views and Belief Systems

Still Other People's Views and Belief Systems

The Common Ground

Photo courtesy of Brandon G. Wilmore

Dr. Jesse McNeil, founder and president of the McNeil Ecumenical Leadership Foundation, says people support what they help create. It is true. This competency is all about getting everyone to work together to develop a vision and goals that they subsequently share and support, because they developed them together. World peace may sound like something contestants in beauty pageants say they are hoping to achieve. I hope they do. But there will likely be more to it than a pretty smile. However, educators working together with their communities do have a real chance or making an impact on society and peace one district at a time. That is what this competency is all about. I love it. It is my very favorite. I hope it will be yours too. If you can nail this one, you can nail the test. Everything else fits under this umbrella of vision.

Go forth, determine your personal vision, plan the goals and steps you will need to take to achieve it, and go do it. Do not sit around wishing any more. Just do it. The difference between success and failure is that one lets adversity get in its way, while the other climbs over adversity to make the world a better place. *That* is the superintendent I want you to be. That is, for sure, the superintendent you are as you are answering questions on this test.

Other words or phrases that test preparers could use instead of stewardship include the following:

- Nurturing
- Sustaining
- Enriching
- Advocating
- Supporting
- Measuring and assessing for improvement

THE SUPERINTENDENT KNOWS HOW TO . . .

- *Establish and support a district culture that promotes learning, high expectations, and academic rigor for self, students, and staff.*

It is one thing to say you promote learning, high expectations, and academic rigors for yourself, students, and staff, but what are you doing that shows it? It must be more than simply talking about it. It must be doing it on a daily basis. Test questions are constructed to see if you realize these things are important by the choices you make.

Please make sure you notice that this competency also holds you to these same high expectations for continuing your own learning, maintaining high expectations for your own performance, and exhibiting rigor in everything you do. Beware of questions that are embedded with the expectation that these issues apply to you as well.

- *Facilitate the development and implementation of a shared vision that focuses on teaching and learning and that ensures the success of all students.*

As discussed in the beginning of this chapter, collaboratively developing, articulating, and implementing a shared vision that focuses on teaching and learning is what the role of the superintendent is all about. It is what you do all day, every day. Figure 4.5 demonstrates how all district goals must support, be aligned with, and lead to the district vision.

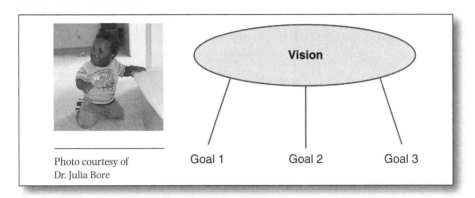

Figure 4.5 Vision and Goal Setting Alignment: All Goals Should Support the District Vision

Photo courtesy of
Dr. Julia Bore

Similarly, Figure 4.6 further shows how all district activities should lead to the success of a targeted goal while all goals continue to lead to attainment of the district vision.

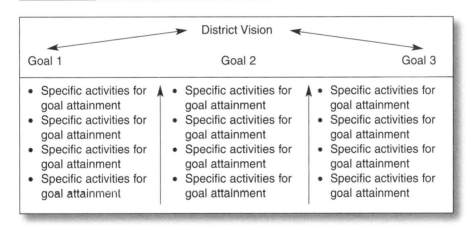

Figure 4.6 District Activities Are Aligned With Specific Goals, Which Lead to the District Vision

Everything the district does should be about ensuring, or guaranteeing, that all students are successful. This include those students with emotional issues, those who move a lot, those who are discipline problems, those who may not have enough to eat or wear, those with learning disabilities, and those whose first language may not remotely resemble English. "All students" means every single one of them. Exactly what will you as superintendent do to ensure the success for each of these students? These are the issues the questions will address with you. Make sure your responses do not exclude anyone, but look to benefit every student.

- *Implement strategies for involving all stakeholders in planning processes and for facilitating planning between constituencies.*

Exactly how are you going to involve all stakeholders, including those whose opinions and philosophies are different from yours, in planning on district issues? How are you going to be the one to facilitate this planning between different constituencies or groups? While it is true that you will have a staff to help you with these things, in the end, it will fall on you. You are the one who will set the stage, the expectations, and will facilitate the district culture and climate to ensure that appropriate planning occurs and that people from all walks of life are included as integral parts of it. Test questions will not ask you to specify what actions you would take in reality. However, they will ask you to select appropriate responses regarding how you would react in fictitious ones. Therefore, as you are reading and selecting the correct response, remember to look for the one that includes all stakeholders and in which you act as the facilitator between different groups. Some of these groups may not agree or even like each other. It will be your role to walk that fine line of problem solver in group-planning processes.

- *Use formal and informal techniques to monitor and assess district and school climate for effective, responsive decision making.*

It isn't easy to develop and maintain a positive district climate that can be used for effective and responsible decision making. So, how will you do this on a regular basis? Is it enough to keep your eyes and ears open to virtually everything that comes up? What formal as well as informal techniques will you use to monitor and assess the climate? In fact, exactly how would you differentiate between formal and informal techniques for doing exactly that?

The key to passing this test is not only to understand the competencies, but also to know how to apply them. In that regard, develop the following:

o Three formal techniques to monitor and assess district climate
o Three informal techniques to monitor and assess district climate
o An explanation of the difference between formal and informal assessment techniques and why you chose each for the situations previously described
o A depiction of a situation you have experienced (or one you have made up) in which monitoring and assessing district climate for

effective, responsive decision making was utilized. Describe how you possibly could have handled it in a different and more productive manner

- *Institute procedures for monitoring the accomplishment of district goals and objectives to achieve the district's vision.*

It is important that you understand that it is the responsibility of the superintendent to make sure there are procedures for monitoring, or staying on top of, the accomplishment of district goals and objectives to achieve the district's vision. Consider the efficacy of these issues:

- o Are our goals directly aligned with our vision to meet the needs of every student?
- o How will we monitor and measure student accomplishment?

If everything we do is to help the district achieve its goals and objectives to get to the vision, exactly what will you as a superintendent do to assess these things? Once the assessments are in place, how will you utilize the results? What potential changes can take place based on the data-driven results?

It is actually a very linear process. As previously shown in Figure 4.6, the vision should have multiple goals and objectives to support it. If it doesn't, it is meaningless rhetoric.

Each goal and objective should subsequently have specific activities and strategies that will ensure they are achieved. Each activity or strategy should have the following:

- o A timeline for accomplishment
- o A mechanism by which it will be assessed
- o Based on assessment results, a process by which strategies can be modified or edited to better facilitate goal attainment
- o Specific resources that are necessary to accomplish the activity or strategy
- o Plans for any staff development necessary to facilitate the attainment of goals that are included in the budget

Remember, it does not matter how good an action plan looks or sounds. What matters is student learning. No matter how much work and effort has gone into planning something, if assessment shows it is not working or it is not maximizing productivity, it is time to make changes. In order to reach the district's vision, many changes in the way things are done and taught will likely have to occur. Change is a necessary part of the improvement process. It is also necessary to take the district from where it is to where it wants to be.

- *Facilitate the development, use, and allocation of all available resources, including human resources, to support implementation of the district's vision and goals.*

Resource procurement and management are essential skills every superintendent must have to facilitate the district reaching its vision. In so doing, we must align the things identified as necessary to reach determined goals and objectives. This skill includes having the right people in the appropriate roles to bring out their best in meeting student needs. It is very difficult, and often impossible, to reach a goal without the necessary people and resources. Therefore, for the district financial plan to be aligned with its vision, all necessary materials, equipment, and personnel must be budgeted for and used in a judicious manner. This alignment is shown in Figure 4.7

Figure 4.7   Budget-Vision Alignment

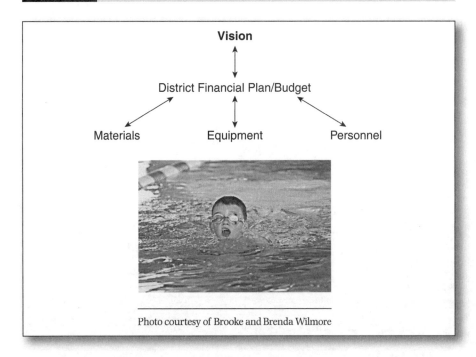

Photo courtesy of Brooke and Brenda Wilmore

- *Recognize and celebrate contributions of staff and community toward realization of the district's vision.*

In supervisory roles, unfortunately it seems human nature to come down on people when they do something wrong. Sometimes corrective feedback is provided. Too often it isn't. Yet it is much rarer to give enough kudos, publicly and privately, when things go right, when someone accomplishes something that was almost impossible, or when a goal is reached that is very rare or unique. In those cases, it is very important to the district culture and climate, as well as vision attainment, for you both to recognize these people's efforts and to celebrate them publicly. The same congratulatory manner should also be given to the community when it has come through on a difficult issue, particularly one that involves potentially raising taxes such as through a bond issue. Another example of celebration should be when solid test scores come in. Everyone should be lauded with more than a onetime, "Gee, fifth-grade reading scores really came up this year. You must have worked really hard." Let your pride in the efforts of campuses, students, families, and the community really show. Let them feel your pride in their accomplishments.

What they have done may not be as big a deal as improved test scores. They could be little things like teachers coming early and staying late to tutor students for no additional pay. That is laudatory behavior and happens very often. There are people who routinely go the extra mile, then another extra mile, to help students have a decent life. Just the right word from you to let them know that you are aware of what they have done, or are doing, can mean so much. When you touch a heart, you touch a life. Celebrate with people when they are happy or have received a blessing. Have empathy with them when they are down. When you do these things, they will come back to you in deepened relationships, trust, and team building toward the district's goals and vision.

- *Maintain awareness of emerging issues and trends affecting public education and communicate their significance to the local educational community.*

As superintendent, it is important for you to stay on top of the news, including current events locally as well as on the state and federal levels. Most of the professional organizations, particularly the American Association of School Administrators, the Texas Association of School Administrators, and the state and national principal organizations do a great job of keeping their members informed electronically and in print about important pending legislation that impacts education. This is just one of many good reasons to be a member. You cannot possibly keep your local community and district aware of current trends and issues if you are not aware of them yourself. You are the voice of education in your district and community. You are the person others expect to speak up about what is going on, how it will impact your district, and if it is a good or a bad idea. Read newspapers and professional journals. Stay in touch with your legislators. Be involved and informed. The profession and society you are seeking to improve is your own.

- *Encourage and model innovative thinking and risk taking and view problems as learning opportunities.*

District improvement will necessitate change. The Seven Last Words of a Decaying School District are, "We never did it that way before." Change precipitates improvement. Without change, we will keep on getting what we have always got. If that is good enough for you, shame on you. We are here to be change agents and to make sure that every student has the best chance possible to receive a free and appropriate education. We can't do that by continuing to operate the way we have always done things, holding steadfastly to the status quo. If we keep on doing what we have always done, we will keep on getting what we have always got. That is not good enough.

A proactive, change-oriented superintendent displays data-based innovative thinking and risk taking on a regular basis while also encouraging others to do likewise. This innovative thinking and risk taking is what will bring about positive change and district improvement. That is what we are all about.

But what happens when a new endeavor is planned, articulated, and implemented (do you recognize the 1–2–3–4 Plan here?), yet it does not turn out well? In fact, it turns into a great big bust. Virtually nothing about it went right.

In those cases, none feel worse than those who are directly involved. They know a bust when they see one. If you come down on them when they are already down, they will never get over it or forget it. In essence, you kicked them when they were down. Who likes that?

Yet the situation cannot be ignored either. What you want to do is turn it into a learning opportunity. Utilize the firm arm with the velvet glove. Talk to those involved from a mentoring perspective. Discuss the situation in a nonthreatening manner. Brainstorm what went wrong, possible causes, and ways a similar disaster could be averted in the future. In essence, use your firm arm to have those involved think it through and brainstorm ways to improve the situation should something similar arise in the future. In this way, you have turned a problem into a learning opportunity. You have turned a bad situation into a great example of the superintendent in a teaching and learning moment. Those are the most gratifying of all. By not being condescending, but approaching it in a firm but helpful manner, you have turned what could have been a relationship derailer into one that builds trust and unity toward the district vision. That is what being an educational leader is all about.

- *Promote multicultural awareness, gender sensitivity, and the appreciation of diversity in the educational community.*

This one is nothing short of beautiful. In fact, it is almost poetic in its beauty. The superintendent is not only the CEO of the school district.

The superintendent's values and dispositions set the culture and climate for the entire district. Therefore, it is of critical importance that you do everything within your capabilities to promote multicultural awareness: that all of us live in the same society together; thus, it is the responsibility of all of us to get to know, understand, and promote cultures other than our own.

The same is equally true of gender sensitivity. Each person, regardless of their sex, is of equal value and must have equal opportunities for academic, athletic, social, extra- and cocurricular, and leadership opportunities. Within classrooms, every occasion must be utilized to meet the needs of all students regardless of their gender, race, or socioeconomic status. Equity continues to be an issue.

Last, there is greater diversity in classrooms and communities than there has been in our history. Remember, diversity is not limited to race. It includes gender, race, mobility, culture, socioeconomics, and so forth. Very importantly, students also have different learning styles, for which there must be adaptations. It is not the responsibility of the students to change their learning styles to make life easier on educators. It is our responsibility to change our teaching and leading styles to best meet their needs. Sometimes it seems like we get that backward. In the districts you lead, make sure everyone knows, understands, and appreciates equity, sensitivity, and the value of diversity.

GUESS MY FAVORITES

It's all about the vision. The vision is everything. Part of that vision is establishing and supporting the district culture. All of this starts at the top with the superintendent.

- Establish and support a district culture that promotes learning, high expectations, and academic rigor for self, students, and staff.
- Facilitate the development and implementation of a shared vision that focuses on teaching and learning and that ensures the success of all students.

IMPORTANT POINTS TO REMEMBER

- It is all about the vision. If something does not relate to the vision, do not waste your time with it.
- The 1–2–3–4 Plan

- Utilize the 1–2–3–4 Plan in *order.* It is not the 3–1–2–4 Plan. It is called the 1–2–3–4 Plan for a reason. Remember that for all questions.
- Collaborate with everyone.
- Diversity is important. Everyone is important
- The educational community consists of everyone.
- People support what they help create.
- Support, encourage, and sustain your people.
- Everyone can be successful provided the right support.
- Formally and informally assess everything all the time for the purpose of making it better.
- Be active and informed professionally.

Learner-Centered Communication and Community Relations

DOMAIN I: Leadership of the Educational Community

DOMAIN KEY CONCEPTS: District Culture, Climate, and Vision

COMPETENCY 003:

> *"The superintendent knows how to communicate and collaborate with families and community members, respond to diverse community interests and needs, and mobilize community resources to ensure educational success for all students."*

This is the competency that specifically addresses how you communicate and collaborate with families and the community. One of the major reasons it is included is to ensure you understand that being a great superintendent is more than being intelligent, certified, and occupying the office. It is being able to interact and converse with district employees and with the greater community as a whole. Your communication skills can make you or they can break you. Remember that sometimes it is not what you say, but how you say it that can make the difference in people's perceptions of things and issues taking place within the district. This applies to both your verbal and your nonverbal skills, as well as to your tone of voice. No matter how "right" you are, sarcasm or a condescending tone will not cut it.

Communication and collaboration go beyond tone and context to content. The district needs to know and see that you are paying attention and responding to their diverse interests and needs. They want to see *how* you are responding: the actions you take are more important to them than the rhetoric you use. Your actions show your true commitment to the diversity within and beyond your district. Lastly, they must be able to see you mobilizing or gathering whatever resources are necessary, to ensure that all students, regardless of backgrounds or disabilities, are able to achieve their maximized success. Many resources are procured beyond the pages of a prescribed budget. They are obtained by creating community partnerships and collaborating with other businesses, civic organizations, churches, and so forth to get or enhance whatever is necessary for the needs of all students.

THE SUPERINTENDENT KNOWS HOW TO . . .

- *Serve as an articulate spokesperson for the importance of public education in a free democratic society.*

You may not need to be quite as articulate as Thomas Jefferson, but coming close would be helpful. It is the role of the superintendent, as it is with all educators, to speak up inside and outside the district about the importance of a quality education that meets the needs of every student. This is a very important concept within a free and democratic society such as ours. As amazing as it may seem to us, there are still countries that stratify their students at a young age. Some students get to continue their educations. Many others do not. In America, we believe that every student deserves a full education and that the public schools are the one vehicle within which every student has that opportunity. There are those who do not understand many of the intricacies of public education, including the reasons why we do certain things for certain students. They are not necessarily trying to be negative or ugly. They simply do not understand our rationale. As superintendent, you are responsible for being the voice for every student. You are the voice for public education as a very important element in a free and democratic society. You may not be Thomas Jefferson, but you are going to give articulating this mission your very best shot anyway . . . especially on the day of the test.

- *Develop and implement an effective and comprehensive internal and external district communications plan and public relations program.*

We just discussed the significance of articulating the value of a free and appropriate education for every student in a democratic society. Yet your role as communicator does not stop with this lofty goal. Each district also must have an internal (for things occurring inside the district) and an external (for district happenings with the community at large) communications plan to make sure that everyone knows everything they need to know at all times. This is often a part of a good public relations program. In larger districts, you will likely have a staff that specializes in public relations and communications. In smaller ones, it is all yours. Regardless, every district must have an internal and external plan in place to articulate to everyone everything that is happening, why it is happening, and their role, if any, in it.

- *Analyze community and district structures and identify major opinion leaders and their relationships to district goals and programs.*

A superintendent once told a new principal that there were few things their board agreed on unanimously. The good news was that they did agree that two citizens were "known nuts" in the community. The bad news was that both citizens had children in the new principal's school. While neither of these citizens carried much credibility around town, they both were good at stirring up the fire and making a lot of smoke, which the superintendent and other administrators subsequently had to deal with. This behavior rapidly had become a nuisance and took the administration's time away from more productive tasks that better related to teaching and learning.

It is important for you to identify who the "major opinion leaders" are as well as their "relationship to district goals and programs." Lyndon Johnson used to say that he wanted to identify exactly who his enemies were so he could keep them close to him. He wanted to keep an eye on them. He also wanted to diffuse any potential problems in a proactive manner, before they got out of hand. Regardless of your political beliefs, none can doubt that Lyndon Johnson met many of his goals. He became president of the United States.

We can learn from him. Sooner or later, every district is going to have someone who is unhappy about something and who becomes quite vocal about it. Instead of waiting for problems to occur then trying to solve them, it is much more positive, as well as time efficient and productive, to seek to develop relationships with "major opinion leaders" such that you can understand what their thinking is and can attempt to clarify it. To do this, you must know and analyze what the community and district structures are so you can determine who is associated with them. The most effective districts are those where the superintendent seeks to develop positive and collaborative relationships with the major community players both inside and outside the school district. Cultivate relationships with the chamber of commerce, major businesses, cultural groups, social service personnel, and any others you can think of.

- *Establish partnerships with families, area businesses, institutions of higher education, and community groups to strengthen programs and support district goals.*

District goals are established as the mechanisms to reach the district vision (Competency 002). Each program and academic unit should have its own goals, which also support district vision attainment. In order for all of this to occur in the most timely and maximized manner, the superintendent must work to establish partnerships with virtually everyone. Beneficial partnerships with families are pretty obvious. Many families are actively engaged in the education of their children, as shown in Figure 5.1. A district priority should be encouraging more family interaction and participation within the schools. This is especially important regarding groups who have not participated in many, if any, campus or district opportunities in the past.

Figure 5.1 Families Are Important in the Education of Their Children

Photo courtesy of John and Beth Hall

We've also previously discussed the benefits of relationships with area businesses and community groups. The new concept introduced this time is "institutions of higher education." What mutual goals can be accomplished by working with community colleges as well as four-year colleges that will be beneficial to everyone? There can be many benefits ranging from dual and concurrent credits to multiple forms of career planning for vocational as well as college-bound students. There are also multiple benefits for district employees to further or enhance their own educations with district partnerships. Virtually all universities have "service" components for their professors. How can your district feed into this "service" in the form of improving teaching and learning? What forms of consulting are available? Utilize your creativity. Meet with university personnel and brainstorm ways each of you can be of service to the other. The establishment of partnerships with institutions of higher education is a win-win as you seek to strengthen district programs as well as to support and to reach goals.

- *Implement effective strategies for systematically communicating with and gathering input from all stakeholders in the district.*

This one is similar to developing and implementing "an effective and comprehensive internal and external district communications plan," but there are distinctions. This example of superintendent performance goes beyond having communications to using the communication systems systematically to gather input, suggestions, and ideas from all facets in the district. So what exactly will you as a superintendent do to develop a system whereby you will *systematically* get input from everyone involved? Think about this and be ready. Questions on the exam will be designed to see if you know that there must be a *systematic* approach as well as that you must be seeking input from *all* members of the community.

- *Communicate and work effectively with diverse social, cultural, ethnic, and racial groups in the district and community so that all students receive appropriate resources and instructional support to ensure educational success.*

There are actually four parts to this very important concept. That's a lot to cover!

o *Communicate and work effectively . . .*

We already understand the importance of communication. Now we are adding working effectively. It doesn't do any good to be communicating far and wide if you aren't accomplishing the goals. For effective work to happen, the superintendent must utilize good skills at listening, drawing forth the opinions of others who are reticent about sharing them, and collaborating with them for the ultimate benefit of achieving the district

Figure 5.2	Highly Successful Superintendents Are Collaborative

- Collaborate With Families and Other Community Members

- Respond to Community Interests and Needs

- Mobilize Community Resources

Photo courtesy of Ryan and Brittani Rollen

vision. Figure 5.2 shows that highly successful superintendents are collaborative with families and other community members, they respond to community interests and needs, and they mobilize community resources to maximize productivity to achieve the district vision. Everything is about achieving the vision.

> o *With diverse social, cultural, ethnic, and racial groups in the district and community so that . . .*

In simple language, communicate and work effectively with *all* groups in the district and community. Do not ignore or slight any of them. Each is equally important.

> o *All students receive appropriate resources and instructional support to . . .*

All of this is done such that every student can have the right resources as well as the instructional support and help necessary for them to be successful. When our students are successful, we are successful. When our students are not successful, we are not successful.

> o *Ensure educational success.*

This is what everything is all about. We are not hoping students will have educational success. We are ensuring, or guaranteeing, that they will do exactly that. We are not just giving lip service to helping every student succeed. We are getting it done.

I told you there was a lot to this one!

- *Develop and use formal and informal techniques to gain an accurate view of the perceptions of district staff, families, and community members.*

Right or wrong, people's perceptions are their reality. Some do not want you to mess up their incorrect perceptions with your facts. They like being "on the dark side." Thankfully, folks like that are not the norm. Most people want to know and understand accurately what is taking place. These perceptions include those of district staff, families, and community members. That is why it is so important that you as the district leader develop and use both formal and informal techniques to make sure your own perceptions of what they think, feel, and know are accurate. Formal techniques may utilize anything from surveys to one-on-one or group discussions. Informal strategies may be more qualitative in nature, such as the conversations you happen upon in which people are talking about an issue. In this way, you learn if they are for or against it or if their understanding of it is correct. Informal strategies are more likely to evolve or just happen. They can even involve your own gut instincts. Formal ones are actually set up to obtain information. Regardless, both are necessary to get a complete picture of perceptions within the district staff, families, and community members. In other words, it is necessary to get a complete picture of *everyone's* perceptions because *everyone* is a part of the school community and is thus a stakeholder.

- *Use effective consensus-building and conflict-management skills.*

Let's clarify terms one more time. *Conflict management* is how you manage disagreements when they occur. Believe me, they will always occur. Although you will do everything possible in a proactive manner to avoid disputes, sometimes they will just happen. Some people simply do not like each other. Some people, believe it or not, may not even like you. Conflict has been with us since antiquity. Conflict management is how you deal with it. From there we transition into consensus building.

Consensus building is what you hope to do when you are bringing different people with diverse ideas and perspectives together to come up with a resolution that everyone can support. It may not have everything in it that everyone wants, but it has enough in it for everyone that the group can support it. Having good consensus-building skills is critically important to the success of your superintendency because, believe it or not, not everyone is going to agree on everything all the time. Sometimes your own staff will not even agree on everything. Your skill in bringing people together to reach consensus can be a major asset to you and your career as you work to improve schools, teaching, and learning.

If all of us had perfect consensus-building and conflict-management skills, there would be peace on earth and goodwill toward men. That would be nice, but right now it isn't happening. As the top district leader, you will come under regular fire for making wrong decisions, even if they are actually right decisions. You will be accused of not being a prudent financial manager, when, it is to be hoped, the opposite is true. You can, and likely will, be accused of virtually anything. And if it isn't you under fire, it is a district employee, program, procedure, or policy. Rest assured someone is always going to be unhappy and creating conflict about something.

There are many consensus-building and conflict-resolution techniques available for you to use. The test will not examine you to make sure you know every one of them. On the contrary, it will be questioning you to make sure you know that you should be using conflict-management and consensus-building techniques rather than exactly which ones they are.

- *Articulate the district's vision and priorities to the community and to the media.*

This one is actually Number 2 in the 1–2–3–4 Plan, which we have referred to several times. In Competency 002, we discussed the extreme importance of the district vision, why it is important, and the significance of articulating it to all stakeholders. This follows up on that same concept with an added facet on the importance of the media. This may come as a shock, but the media aren't always your best friend. They are in business to make money, not to educate students. The way they make money is to present news that sells. The fact that your parents are wonderful volunteers is nice news, but it doesn't necessarily create a stir (otherwise known as selling newspapers or generating television and radio ratings) in the community. They can save your parent volunteer story for a slow news day.

What they want are unusual things that will capture people's attention. If someone with a gun shows up on a district campus and proceeds to use it, that is news. It will sell papers and have all sorts of people glued to their media outlets. No one can blame them. The public does have a right to know.

However, what you can do is to be proactive in your relationships with media outlets. Make sure they really understand the district vision, goals, and means by which the district plans to attain them. Think of this relationship building as putting money in a savings account. You may not need it at this moment, but

- o you want it working for you, not against you, and
- o you want it in case of emergency.

We do want to use the media wisely. We want them to help us clearly articulate our vision. However, when things happen that are less than desirable, we also want them there to help us communicate it accurately and without bias. This is a collaborative partnership. They need us because we are newsmakers. We need them to help us articulate our vision and everything else that happens in the district appropriately.

- *Influence the media by using proactive communication strategies that serve to enhance and promote the district's vision.*

We have basically covered the main parts of this bullet earlier. Of course, we want to utilize proactive communication strategies with the media to enhance and promote the district's vision. However, we also want to work closely with the media, to use proactive communication strategies, and to encourage them to use their media resources in ways that help us promote the district vision rather than ways that can damage it. Sometimes this is easier said than done.

- *Communicate effectively about positions on educational issues.*

This one is very similar to the first bullet, which read, "Serve as an articulate spokesperson for the importance of public education in a free democratic society." This time, in addition to being that spokesperson for the larger idea of education, you are effectively conveying the district's and your position on educational issues. These issues could range from a local bond election or the decision to build a new athletic or fine arts complex to issues before the state legislature or coming before Congress. Whether the topic is a relatively minor local issue or a broader federal policy, as superintendent you must communicate effectively about positions on all educational issues. That covers a lot of ground and a lot of issues.

- *Use effective and forceful writing, speaking, and active listening skills.*

This bullet is an excellent summary to all of the above bullets. In order for you to be the master communicator that Competency 003 wants you to be, you must exercise your communication skills in every arena.

- *Writing:* You are representing the district with every word you write. This may sound obvious, but make sure you proof everything you send out. Run spell-check. Check your grammar and punctuation. Do your subjects and verbs agree? Most of us have seen the horror stories of written works schools have sent home that parents have sent back corrected. That is totally embarrassing. Please do not let it happen to you. It makes you look bad and the district look worse. Make sure your writing makes its points in a forceful, effective, accurate, coherent, and well-written manner.

- *Speaking:* All of the preceding is also true when you are speaking. Speak in a professional manner. Be accurate, coherent, and succinct. Identify with people through the choice of your words, phrases, and mannerisms. Sell the district and its vision in both formal and informal ways.

Everything you say and do is being judged by someone. You are never really alone and absolutely nothing is "off the record." As you speak, and in everything else you do, make sure you are speaking with "integrity, fairness, and in an ethical manner" (Competency 001). Any accidental slipups that may occur can, and likely will, come back to haunt you.

o *Active listening skills:* There is a difference between half-listening to a person or group and actively listening to them. Listen with your full attention on whoever is speaking. Give their thoughts respect and consideration. Do not make decisions until you know all the facts. Be sincere and genuine. Others will sense when you are not and may become more unhappy than they were to begin with. Everyone deserves respect. Give it to them, and then hope they return the favor in a like manner.

GUESS MY FAVORITES

In many ways, my favorites for Competency 003 are a broader representation of my favorites for Competencies 001 and 002. Without a clearly articulated district vision and established priorities, the district will not maximize its effectiveness in the greater school community. These are the basic premises upon which public education in America is based. A solid education is a mandate for every student. The superintendent is the focal individual upon which this responsibility lies.

- Serve as an articulate spokesperson for the importance of public education in a free democratic society.
- Articulate the district's vision and priorities to the community and to the media.

IMPORTANT POINTS TO REMEMBER

- Be the best spokesperson anyone has ever dreamed of, and speak for the district and everyone in it.
- Communicate with everyone with respect, consideration, and courtesy.
- Seek to establish effective partnerships with virtually everyone and every group.
- Work with the community to get the nonbudgeted resources necessary for students to succeed. These resources may range from shoes to eyeglasses to afterschool child care. Whatever it is, work to get it.
- Be a consensus builder, not a divider.

Learner-Centered Contexts

DOMAIN I: Instructional Leadership

DOMAIN KEY CONCEPTS: District Culture, Climate, and Vision

COMPETENCY 004:

> *"The superintendent knows how to respond to and influence the larger political, social, economic, legal, and cultural context, including working with the board of trustees, to achieve the district's educational vision."*

Some people entering school leadership do not realize that their roles go beyond the internal and external leadership of the district all the way to the "larger political, social, economic, legal, and cultural context[s]" within which they function. This competency, in essence, is saying that superintendents become activists for the district's vision. Once you have covered the "larger political, social, economic, legal, and cultural context," you have, in essence, covered all the contexts there are, including working with the board of trustees. Remember, when your board is happy, you are happy. When your board is *not* happy . . . well, you can guess what that can mean. The hard part is making sure it is happy and doing the right things at the right times. That is where your contextual and activist role comes in.

THE SUPERINTENDENT KNOWS HOW TO . . .

- *Analyze and respond to political, social, economic, and cultural factors affecting students and education.*

Political, social, economic, and cultural factors cover just about everything that could affect students and education. Figure 6.1 puts in visual perspective the way an ongoing cycle is formed. The legislature sets new laws and regulations, which impact schools and districts. As superintendent, you must be constantly aware of what these are as well as their impact on your district and community.

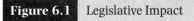

Figure 6.1   Legislative Impact

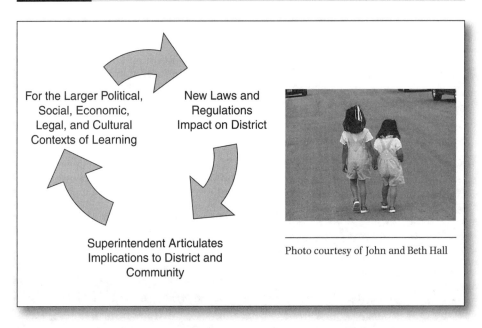

For the Larger Political, Social, Economic, Legal, and Cultural Contexts of Learning

New Laws and Regulations Impact on District

Superintendent Articulates Implications to District and Community

Photo courtesy of John and Beth Hall

You then exercise Number 2 of the 1–2–3–4 Plan by clearly articulating all of this, both the laws and their potential impact, to everyone internal and external to the district. These factors, in turn, drive the larger political, social, economic, legal, and cultural contexts of your district and all others. As these factors or issues settle into reality, the cycle continues by starting all over and doing it again. Thus, as superintendent you will constantly be analyzing, as well as responding to, current events and all other factors. Virtually anything can, and likely will, impact student learning. Family problems? Impact learning. Attacks on America as in September 11, 2001? Definitely impact learning. Does a student or family not have enough food? Yes, that has a real impact on learning. Every decision has more far-reaching implications than you might think. Figure 6.2 shows the cyclical nature of contexts, laws, regulations, and their impacts on the way the district functions from the highly important legislative perspective. This cyclical nature reinforces why you must be actively engaged with your legislators on both the state and federal levels. The ways they vote will have financial and other impacts on the district(s) you lead. It is well to your advantage to network amongst them and at all times to be serving as an advocate for the district and the students therein.

Figure 6.2 Let the Legislative Fun Begin

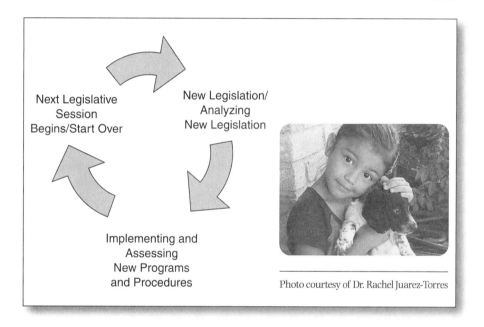

Photo courtesy of Dr. Rachel Juarez-Torres

You know these things, and you know you must respond to them. How will you

- o analyze what their impacts will be,
- o respond to their effects, and
- o utilize the results?

- • *Provide leadership in defining superintendent and board roles and establishing mutual expectations.*

It will be your responsibility to lead the board members in defining their roles (development of policy) and your role (implementing it through daily operation of the district). Together, you must develop mutual expectations, goals, and measurements. While this may sound like a lot of trouble while the ink is still wet on your contract, it will come back to be of benefit to all of you each year as your evaluation rolls around. Set collaborative goals where each of you understands what is expected. Make especially sure that your goals are measurable. Measurable goals can protect you if any board member suddenly decides your performance is not where it should be. At the same time, be sure to schedule time for team-building exercises between you and them that incorporate district goal development and specific ways each of you will be of benefit. Defining mutual expectations will definitely be of mutual long-term benefit.

- *Communicate and work effectively with board members in varied contexts, including problem-solving and decision-making contexts.*

The very best districts are those whose superintendents and boards work closely together in every circumstance to solve problems and make decisions that are in the best interest of teaching and learning. In order for those things to happen, good communication is essential between each person in every context. Student learning will be maximized when each stakeholder is able to work productively, with needed resources, and with individual student needs and learning styles in mind. For this to occur, you must lead in communicating and working effectively with board members in all arenas including problem-solving and decision-making contexts.

- *Work with the board of trustees to define mutual expectations, policies, and standards.*

Similar to setting mutual expectations between the superintendent and board is defining exactly what those expectations mean. This also applies to setting district policies and establishing standards for academics and every other area of district life. It all comes down to working closely with the board on every issue. Define the district vision, then work together to turn it into reality.

- *Access and work with local, state, and national political systems and organizations to elicit input on critical educational issues.*

Being actively engaged as the educational leader of the district and community is not enough. Forward-thinking superintendents go beyond local boundaries to state and national political arenas and organizations. Stay in close contact with those in decision-making positions that could impact public education in general and your district specifically. As demonstrated in Figures 6.1 and 6.2, the legislature is of critical importance in shaping the future of school districts. The professional organizations are an excellent tool to utilize to achieve the goal of targeted focus, and you might consider the benefits of lobbying with them. The strength that comes from large numbers of administrators bound together to address common causes cannot be underestimated. The American Association of School Administrators sends regular legislative e-mail updates to members, makes suggestions of whom to contact regarding pending legislation, and does research on virtually every educational issue imaginable. The Texas Association of School Administrators, as well as the state and national principal organizations, functions in like manner. These organizations exist for the purpose of helping you help others. Join the appropriate organization, utilize its resources, and develop it for the benefit of your district.

- *Use legal guidelines to protect the rights of students and staff and to improve learning opportunities.*

This is an example of how the TExES exam will direct legal questions to you. They may insert answer choices that are illegal. If you pick them, they will know you do not know the legal guidelines that have been established to protect the rights of students and staff and to improve learning opportunities. Examples of this method of detection are in questions regarding application of IDEA issues, FERPA, and the use of social security numbers. If ever in doubt, in real life or on the test, err on the side of caution. Never take the chance of violating anyone's rights or privacy. Keep everything legal, moral, and ethical. Pick answers on the test that ensure these things will happen.

- *Prepare and recommend district policies to improve student learning and district performance in compliance with state and federal requirements.*

It is part of your responsibility as superintendent to prepare and make recommendations to the board for policies that will be legal, are in compliance with state and federal requirements, and are designed to improve student learning. It is the board's job to ask reflective as well as data-driven questions and to focus policy. Critical thinking and respectful brainstorming of ideas from the board, the administrative team, and the district community should seek to engage expanded thought to improve teaching and learning. In every instance, you must ensure the district is in compliance with the myriad of state and federal requirements for everything from No Child Left Behind to the Free and Reduced-Priced Lunch Program. There are no exceptions. Every single issue must be legal and in compliance. If they are not, they will be discovered. That won't be pretty, so do not go there. Keep the focus of the district on improving student learning. Keep everything else in line and always ensure everything is done in a legal and ethical manner.

GUESS MY FAVORITES

This competency centers, in large part, on the superintendent-board relationship. Improving student learning must always be a top priority. In order for that to occur, there must be respect and understanding of the roles and expectations of both the superintendent and the board.

- Provide leadership in defining superintendent–board roles and establishing mutual expectations.
- Prepare and recommend district policies to improve student learning and district performance in compliance with state and federal requirements.

IMPORTANT POINTS TO REMEMBER

- The school board is the boss. Work with the members. Do not order them around. Educate them on defining roles and boundaries for each of you.
- Keep the school board knowledgeable about things that happen in the district. They do not want to hear it secondhand.
- Be on full red alert to respond to anything and everything.
- Everything that happens could, and likely will, end up relating to education.
- If a policy is in effect, use it. If it isn't appropriate, work to get it changed. Until then, use it.
- Keep everything legal and above reproach.

Learner-Centered Strategic Planning

DOMAIN II: Instructional Leadership

DOMAIN KEY CONCEPTS: Curriculum, Instruction, and Staff Development

COMPETENCY 005:

> *"The superintendent knows how to facilitate the planning and implementation of strategic plans that enhance teaching and learning; ensure alignment among curriculum, curriculum resources, and assessment; and promote the use of varied assessments to measure student performance."*

We have now transitioned from Domain I, where the focus was on the district culture, climate, and vision, to Domain II, where the focus is on curriculum, instruction, and staff development. While each competency in the entire test will in some way still address the district culture, climate, and vision, from here on, their primary issues will be on other things. Continue to think of the district culture, climate, and vision as the big umbrella of district leadership. The competencies from here on are the spokes that help support, or hold up, the big umbrella of the district's culture, climate, and vision.

Competency 005 primarily addresses the importance of strategic planning, alignment, and assessment of everything the district does. Do you remember the 1–2–3–4 Plan (Figure 4.2) from Competency 002?

Let's apply it now to the issues of strategic planning, alignment, and assessment. First, we start with Number 1, development. In this case, we are strategically planning everything the district does to enhance teaching and learning. We are also developing and planning how we will align district curriculum with the resources needed to support and enhance the curriculum as well as how we will assess it. We want to collaborate in this strategic planning with as many diverse stakeholders as possible because

- there is strength in diversity of opinions and inputs,
- people support what they help create, and,
- therefore, collaboration is a good thing.

In the 1–2–3–4 Plan, we would next utilize Number 2, which is articulating exactly how each of these things is going to occur. There will be strength and help in this process because you will incorporate the assistance of all the same people who were involved in Number 1 in the articulation of Number 2. It all fits together in a cyclical pattern that continues to spread outwards into the rest of the district, just as a stone tossed in a lake creates concentric ripples outward. Therefore, the more that developers and supporters of district plans talk to their own friends, families, neighbors, and so forth, the more far-reaching benefits their collaboration will generate. All of these people together will have a wider and more in-depth outreach than you and your leadership team alone could possibly ever have.

Next, in Number 3, we implement whatever the plans are because now, it is to be hoped, the district knows and understands what it is the plans are for, why they are necessary and important, and the district's special roles in the accomplishment of those plans. Finally, Number 4, we must always be good stewards of district time, money, and efficiency. Therefore, we must assess everything we do in various ways that will measure student performance, and everything else, within their appropriate levels.

THE SUPERINTENDENT KNOWS HOW TO . . .

- *Facilitate effective curricular decision making based on an understanding of pedagogy, curriculum design, cognitive development, learning processes, and child and adolescent growth and development.*

Decisions you make about curriculum should be based on solid research concerning child and adolescent growth and development such as those presented in Jean Piaget's cognitive development process of developmental psychology. Different individuals progress through different developmental states at different points. Therefore, curriculum that is appropriate for one child, or age span, may or may not be effective for another. Although it may seem too idealistic to be practical, the Ideal Superintendent leads curricular improvement that is based on understanding good teaching practices (pedagogy), the way individuals learn (learning processes), proper design within the curriculum itself, as well as understanding of cognitive development. Each of these elements should be integrated together to produce curriculum that is student based.

- *Implement planning procedures to develop curricula that achieve optimal student learning and that anticipate and respond to occupational and economic trends.*

Society is changing, thus, so is the world and everyone in it. The students we have today are different, and have far different needs, from those as recent as a generation ago. Different occupational and economic trends are in play today that did not exist before. We are no longer a primarily agricultural society. Although there are still many jobs available in industry, the work place is changing there also. More service-oriented and technological jobs need workers today to fill their ever-increasing roles in society. Because of that trend, school districts must also change to keep up, much less stay ahead, of the changing times and workplace. This obligation includes having the organizational foresight to look ahead, anticipate, and respond to occupational and economic trends. As superintendent, it is your responsibility to lead and implement planning procedures that will help develop and enhance curricula by which students can optimize their learning capacities.

- *Implement core curriculum design and delivery systems to ensure instructional quality and continuity across the district.*

Within every district there will, or should, be core curriculum that feeds into a systemwide scope and sequence of what concepts are taught and when. In Texas, this is currently often TAKS-driven as teachers work feverishly to prepare students for what they will encounter in these high-stakes tests.

Whether questions presented to you will relate to TAKS or any other testing tool (achievement tests, scores, trends, etc.), your focus should not be the test itself. Your focus should be how your district is ensuring that the curriculum itself as well as the instructional paths and delivery systems utilized are designed from the perspective of ensuring quality and a consistent flow of instruction vertically and horizontally in the district. Obviously, as superintendent, you will not likely be directly involved in the nuts and bolts of actual curriculum development unless you are in a very, very small district. Do not fall into the trap that curriculum and instruction are not under your purview. They most definitely are. You lead, manage, and supervise those that do these incredibly important "meat and potatoes" jobs in the district. Your role remains to "advocate, nurture, and sustain an instructional program" (Competency 006) as well as to monitor and evaluate it in the district you serve. The primary distinctive factor between school districts and other organizations is that of education. Education is made up of curriculum (what we teach) and instruction (how we teach it). Other organizations may have culture, climate, and vision (Domain I). They have finance, facilities, and safety issues (Domain III). They may even have professional development responsibilities (Domain II). But only education has a primary focus on teaching and learning as a result of curriculum and instruction.

- *Develop and implement collaborative processes for systematically assessing and renewing the curriculum to meet the needs of all students and ensure appropriate scope, sequence, content, and alignment.*

In the previous bullet, the focus was on implementing curricular design and delivery systems for the purpose of ensuring instructional quality and continuity across the district. This bullet goes a step further in the process of developing (creating) and implementing (putting into place) a collaborative process whereby many stakeholders take part and offer input for systematically (consistently across the school system) assessing and renewing (improving or enhancing) the curriculum. Again, these are segments from the 1–2–3–4 Plan (Competency 002 and throughout) as shown in Figure 4.2.

This process exists to make sure (ensure) that the curricular needs of all (every one of them) students are being met. The process must also move forward to include how it will ensure (guarantee) appropriate scope, sequence, content, and alignment of everything that is being taught. All together, these things make this a very important bullet. You will see exactly how important it is when you Guess My Favorites below.

- *Use assessment to measure student learning and diagnose student needs to ensure educational accountability.*

There are many varied ways to assess student learning and to diagnose their needs. Many of them are done informally by teachers and others interacting with students every day. They are done without formalized testing. However, what gets measured gets done. That does *not* mean we must test everything all day, every day, all year. We already have way too much pressure put on teachers about high-stakes testing. This bullet is not intended to add more to it. It is saying that assessment (formal and informal) is important to see how students are progressing in their learning. It is also important for educational accountability purposes.

If the high-stakes testing craze we are currently experiencing went away tomorrow, we would still have educational accountability. What it could look like is not our purpose here. However, as a tax-funded entity, school districts use a lot of money. The public does have a right to know how this money is being spent and that they are getting good "bang for their buck" in the educational arena.

- *Evaluate district curricula and provide direction for improving curricula based on sound, research-based practices.*

All of our curriculum should be based and evaluated on sound, research-based practices. As shown in Figure 7.1, research-based curriculum evaluation leads to a research-based curriculum. This, in turn, directly correlates to improved student learning, which leads directly to the district vision. It's a no-brainer. Make sure all programs, curriculum, and decisions are research based.

The test will not be asking you to identify specific research practices or theories. They will expect you to know and demonstrate in selection of answer choices that the curriculum we use, the instructional strategies utilized, and the method by which they are evaluated, all must be research-based. Be sure to remember that when you are making answer selections. If an answer isn't research based, do not pick it!

Figure 7.1   Research-Based District Movement

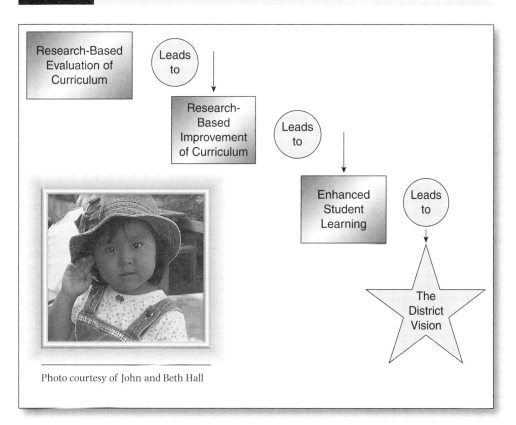

Photo courtesy of John and Beth Hall

- *Integrate the use of technology, telecommunications, and information systems into the school district curriculum to enhance learning for all students.*

Technology utilized in districts today is there to enhance student learning, not drive it. It is there to enhance the operating efficiency of the district and campus offices, not frustrate people. Make sure technology is integrated throughout the district everywhere from classrooms to offices to off-campus sites. In addition, telecommunications and information systems should be used to "advocate, nurture, and sustain" (Competency 006) district programs for the purpose of enhancing student learning.

- *Facilitate the use of creative thinking, critical thinking, and problem solving by staff and other school district stakeholders involved in curriculum design and delivery.*

As long as we keep on doing what we have always done with curriculum design and delivery (instruction), we will keep on getting what we have always got. Is student performance good enough in your district that you feel confident that doing the same things over and over is good enough? Unless every student in your entire district is learning to their maximized capacity, motivated beyond all reason, and doing magnificently well, then we must be facilitating creative thinking, critical thinking, and other forms of problem solving by virtually everyone involved with teaching and learning. This does include the community itself. Get out of the box. Forget the box. Find new ways to do things that can produce results with those who have yet to be successful. We can't do this while hanging on to "the way we used to do things." Yesterday is not coming back. Today, with today's students, is here. It is our job to get everyone involved out of the box, brainstorming new ideas, and trying new strategies to improve teaching and learning for all students. Thus, creative thinking, critical thinking, and problem solving are tools to enhance, enrich, and improve curriculum design (development of appropriate and differentiated curriculum) and delivery (appropriate instructional strategies) for greater student learning.

- *Facilitate the effective coordination of district and campus curricular and extracurricular programs.*

In most districts, it is not your job to make sure the band has buses to ride to out-of-town football games. However, it is your job to facilitate that all district and campus curricular *and extracurricular* programs are coordinated, where everyone has what they need to teach and learn, and for students to be able to be successful. So while it may not be your specific responsibility to line up the buses, it is your responsibility to coordinate that everything that happens in the district is organized in an efficient, effective, and timely manner.

GUESS MY FAVORITES

The focus of Domain I was the district culture, climate, and vision. Now, in Domain II, the focus has changed to curriculum, instruction, and professional development. The superintendent must be the facilitator of collaborative planning processes to make sure that everything related to each of these is appropriate, assessed, modified, and aligned. In order for these things to occur and flourish within the district, creative thinking, critical thinking, and problem solving are essentials.

- Develop and implement collaborative processes for systematically assessing and renewing the curriculum to meet the needs of all students and ensure appropriate scope, sequence, content, and alignment.
- Facilitate the use of creative thinking, critical thinking, and problem solving by staff and other school district stakeholders involved in curriculum design and delivery.

IMPORTANT POINTS TO REMEMBER

- Your primary role is to improve teaching and learning.
- Align everything: vision, goals, budget, staff development, assessment, everything.
- Decisions and practices must be research based.
- Continuously monitor, assess, and modify everything to improve student learning.
- Be accountable.
- Think and act collaboratively, creatively, and critically to invest stakeholders and to improve student learning. Everything is to improve student learning.

Learner-Centered Instructional Leadership and Management

DOMAIN II: Instructional Leadership

DOMAIN KEY CONCEPTS: Curriculum, Instruction, and Staff Development

COMPETENCY 006:

> *"The superintendent knows how to advocate, nurture, and sustain an instructional program and a district culture that are conducive to student learning and staff professional growth."*

We discussed the district culture and stewardship of the vision in Domain I, Competency 002. However, many of the competencies tend to overlap in function. Nowhere is that more evident than in 006, in which it states, "The superintendent knows how to advocate, nurture, and sustain an instructional program and a district culture that are conducive to student learning and staff professional growth." Therefore, what we are doing with 006 is merely continuing with variations on themes we have already discussed, but they are now spun a different direction.

As shown in Figure 8.1, in Competency 006, we are still looking strongly at the district culture as we were in 002. However, this time we are not focusing on the district vision as we previously were. We are now looking at how the district culture influences, supports, and helps

Figure 8.1	Highly Successful Superintendents Provide Instructional Leadership

- Promoting a Positive School Culture

- Providing an Effective Instructional Program

- Appling Best Practices for Student Learning

- Designing Comprehensive Professional Growth Plans

Photo courtesy of Lee and Alison Hefley

(i.e., "advocates, nurtures, and sustains") student learning and staff professional growth. Everything we do should be about supporting and enhancing student performance. In order for this to occur, we must continuously provide and encourage all staff to grow and learn through individual, campus, and district professional development opportunities that are aligned with student needs as well as campus and district goals. Remember: As superintendent, you are part of the staff. Just because you have finished your degree, passed the TExES exam, and gotten your dream job as a superintendent does not mean your personal learning and growing are over. In fact, it is quite the contrary. Superintendents must model lifelong learning to the entire staff as well as to the district at large. This is necessary both to keep growing yourself and to have credibility with others. This can be done in various ways including researching best practices and innovations, the development and implementation of new teaching and learning theories, and improved technologies to increase teaching and learning. Models for accomplishing these goals include conducting research on the Internet, taking online courses, participating in reading and book study groups, taking additional graduate course work, participating in activities sponsored by Education Region Service Centers, and attending the multitude of wonderful seminars, conferences, and research sponsored by the professional organizations. In Texas, the Texas Association of School Administrators

(TASA) is the primary superintendent professional organization. TASA sponsors many conferences across the state including the fall annual conference in conjunction with the Texas Association of School Boards (TASB), the midwinter administrators' conference, and others. In recent years, the Summer Seminar, in which superintendents and trustees attend together as a "Team of 8," has become increasingly popular. In the end, as we said in 001, actions speak louder than words. By actively engaging in visible personal professional development, we are ethically modeling the behaviors we want others to emulate. Superintendents, thus, are the head leaders of learners.

There is one more thing we really need to refocus on before going into the bullets below. That is the issue of advocating, nurturing, and sustaining instruction and professional development. In 002, we discussed the concept of stewardship. There is no better definition of stewardship in terms of the superintendent than advocating, nurturing, and sustaining just about everything going on. Superintendents are facilitators of the successful accomplishment of all things that occur within a district. They are the "master facilitators." As such, it is not your job to do everything. It is your job to make sure everything gets done efficiently, effectively, and in a safe, supportive culture and climate. Virtually everyone achieves more when they are supported and sustained, when they feel free to take risks to improve the district, and when creativity as well as accountability are valued. This is the kind of district culture that you want to create. It is also the philosophy behind many of the correct responses on the test. Do not pick answers based on reality or on what you have seen someone else do. Base your responses on the ideal response to create the ideal situation. Ideal responses are always the ones that "advocate, nurture, and sustain" whatever is in question.

THE SUPERINTENDENT KNOWS HOW TO . . .

- *Apply knowledge of motivational theories to create conditions that encourage staff, students, families or caregivers, and the community to strive to achieve the district's vision.*

Superintendents must be encouragers of all others in the district. It makes no difference if it is to other administrators, teachers, staff, parents or caregivers, community members, or students. It is your job to be the "first face" and the "first voice" in regard to achieving the district's vision. This again refers back to the strategic planning and alignment process discussed in Chapter 4, Competency 002. It is your job to create the conditions (i.e., culture and climate) so that all members of the district learning community have the knowledge, skills, and resources necessary to achieve the vision that was previously collaboratively developed, articulated, implemented, and ultimately evaluated as described and shown in Figure 8.1.

In these ways, the superintendent is the Grand Encourager in Action, seeking to demonstrate through modeled behavior the belief that every student's needs will be met through developmentally appropriate curriculum and instruction.

- *Facilitate the implementation of sound, research-based theories and techniques of classroom management, student discipline, and school safety to ensure a school district environment conducive to learning.*

This is a good example of the utilization of the word *facilitate*. It is not saying that it is your job to be The One who knows all there is to know about the "sound, research-based theories and techniques" previously described. Rather, it is here to remind us that classroom management, student discipline, and school safety are critical attributes in having a district environment (i.e., culture and climate) that is conducive to and ensures maximized student learning. Therefore, while it is not necessarily your role to be an expert on each of these, it is your role as facilitator to ensure there are district personnel who are experts in each and that the 1–2–3–4 Plan is utilized in the development, articulation, implementation, and evaluation and stewardship of policies, resources, assessment, and organizational oversight of each.

- *Facilitate the development of a learning organization that encourages educational excellence, supports instructional improvement, and incorporates best practice.*

A key concept in mega-achieving classrooms, campuses, and districts is setting high standards and expectations for everything that occurs. Each is a learning and growing subgroup within the global district organization. Any organization must have a continuous influx of new ideas and best practices or it will begin to deteriorate. It has been said that the worst enemy of a good organization is being pretty good. There is a tendency of pretty good organizations to cut back on continuous assessment, to stop focusing as strenuously on creative new ideas and the passionate pursuit of excellence. The quest should be for improvement 100% of the time by asking how to do every single thing better and constantly assessing what is being done to reach district and campus goals. If an activity or strategy that has previously been agreed upon and implemented is not being successful, change it. Don't wait till the end of the year to look at program and personnel effectiveness. Lead the district (i.e., learning organization) in a quest for excellence through assessment on a continuing and day-to-day basis. If the horse is dead, get off. If something is not being effective, change it.

How can we make everything better when the concept sounds over-whelming? A major error educational leaders, as well as leaders from other organizations, make is a lack of ongoing assessment. How can we improve something if we do not know the facts through cold hard data of what is being accomplished, if it is effective, and at what cost? Therefore, for a learning organization (i.e., district) to improve, the superintendent must encourage and demand excellence in every facet of the district, sup-port creativity and research-based risk taking to support instructional improvement, and be constantly vigilant that best practices are utilized and regularly evaluated.

- *Facilitate the ongoing study of current best practice and relevant research and encourage the application of this knowledge to district and school improvement initiatives.*

This bullet transitions nicely from the one preceding it. As superin-tendent, you may, or may not, be the most conversant district person with regard to current best practice and relevant research. Frankly, I hope you are. It shows you have the inner core of expertise and credibility necessary to maximize your effectiveness as an educational leader and role model.

However, it is possible that you may not be the district's top expert in every area. In this case, it is particularly important that you surround yourself with personnel, with leaders, who are experts in each facet. You then provide the oversight and support necessary for them to be efficient and effective in their roles in school and district improvement initiatives. While simultaneously researching and analyzing current best practice and research relevant to the district, you, your role, are to encourage the application of all of this throughout the district and to advocate, nurture, and sustain others to do likewise.

- *Plan and manage student services and activity programs to address devel-opmental, scholastic, social, emotional, cultural, physical, and leadership needs.*

This is one of those bullets where the developers sought to make sure they included every possible student need. Therefore, conceivably, you could edit it to read, "Plan and manage *everything* to address *all* student needs." Sure, it would be less wordy. But it also may not clarify for you exactly what they mean by *everything* and *all.* Consequently, they spell out all the details.

Nonetheless, as shown in Figure 8.2, we must understand that the super-intendent is the person ultimately responsible that *all* (i.e., developmental,

Figure 8.2	All Programs Should Be Needs Based

Student Services and Activity Programs

- Developmental
- Scholastic
- Social
- Emotional
- Cultural
- Physical
- Leadership Needs

Photo courtesy of Jennifer and Brian Williams

scholastic, social, emotional, cultural, physical, leadership) needs of *all* students actually are being met. While this may not sound like a realistic expectation, remember that these competencies were not based on reality.

They are based on determining your understanding of what an Ideal Superintendent should know and be able to do so that when you actually become a superintendent, you will have a clear understanding of the high leadership expectations placed on you. If you do not know what ideal looks like (student services, activity programs, academics, athletics, fine arts, cocurricular, etc.), how could you facilitate the development of a mission, goals, and strategies to lead the district to attain them?

- *Establish a comprehensive school district program of student assessment, interpretation of data, and reporting of state and national data results.*

This is a critically important bullet. A case could be made that it is one of the most important within all ten competencies. The reason for its high importance is the focus on "student assessment, interpretation of data, and reporting" of all of it in relation to state and national standards, policies, regulations, and reports. We are faced with varying circumstances. Some districts have a multitude of data, which they could analyze, interpret, and utilize for campus and district improvement, yet they do not maximize its utilization properly. Perhaps they do not know how and need your help in teaching them or bringing in someone who can. Thus, they are not getting the entire "bang for their buck" from district resources, including the finances and personnel, to get all of the implications and results that they could from the data. In other words, they are not maximizing productivity from the data they have already collected.

In other instances, there are districts that may not know how to obtain or organize assessment data beyond that provided through the Texas Assessment of Knowledge and Skills (TAKS) and Academic Excellence Indicator System (AEIS) reports. Then there are some who do not appropriately disaggregate the data presented in even these reports, consequently resulting in not being able to make the most of what they have to improve teaching and learning. Subsequently, they are not able to align staff development and resources with actual student needs, nor do they know how to appropriately articulate the results toward state and national standards in oral, written, or online ways in which the school community (teachers, staff, parents or caregivers, media, students, etc.) can understand and support what is being presented to them, its implications, and what it all means to them.

This bullet was written to address all of these issues. The point here is that all districts must collaboratively decide exactly what types of data they need, as well as how to obtain, organize, synthesize, summarize, and draw conclusions from them to best enhance curriculum, instructional strategies, teacher efficacy, and student learning. Without a thorough analysis of data, informed and prudent decision making cannot occur. The importance of data analysis is emphasized throughout the standards. We will address a variation of it in the eighth bullet of this competency then again in detail in Domain III, Competency 010. The second bullet of 010 says, "Implement processes for gathering, analyzing, and using data for informed decision making." Folks, let me tell you something. When the developers of these competencies so strongly emphasize the same ideas in more than one domain, that is a hint. They think data-driven decision making is very important or they would not have focused on it twice and referred to it more than that. They are strong on this concept. You should be also. Therefore, think smart. Watch for questions and answers that address these issues. They like utilization of data-driven decision making to maximize district, campus, and student success. Therefore, they will have questions on the test to address your understanding of these concepts. Watch for these questions, and chose your responses accordingly.

- *Apply knowledge of special programs to ensure that students with special needs are provided with appropriate resources and effective, flexible instructional programs and services.*

A simplified way of writing this bullet could be, "*Apply* (not just *know*, but *apply*, which is a higher level operation) knowledge of *everything* (all programs including academic, athletic, cognitive, social, cultural, etc.) to ensure that *all* (i.e., those with special needs and everyone else) students are provided with everything they need (i.e., appropriate resources and effective, flexible instructional programs and services) to be successful. Special needs students will indeed need some things, including increased personnel and instructional, curricular, and assessment modifications, to help them learn and be successful. But the principle here is the same for every student. All of them, including the special needs students, English language learners, culturally diverse students, and so forth, need, deserve, and must have the individual attention, tools and instructional strategies that meet their physical, emotional, and learning styles. Anything less is not enough. If this sounds like a Pollyanna approach to district leadership, fine. Call me Pollyanna. We already have enough cynics in the world who are negative about too many things. Students, each and every one, deserve access to everything they need to become all they can be. This will often mean personalized curriculum, modified assignments, different instructional approaches, diverse forms of assessment, individualized planning, and anything else necessary to provide flexible instructional programs and services for anyone who needs it.

- *Analyze instructional resource needs and deploy instructional resources effectively and equitably to enhance student learning.*

The bullet does not say to deploy instructional resources effectively and "equally" to enhance student learning. The word used is "equitably." Sometimes the two are not the same. Here is an example.

When I was a school board trustee, often issues would come up where another board member would have difficulty understanding why some students were entitled to have additional resources, including bus transportation, when all students were not given the same "special favors." There were those who felt that it "wasn't fair" for some students to be given privileges that all students could not have. In one instance, another board member, who was also a friend, was particularly confused. Finally, I provided him an example that was close to home. I knew, and had been principal for, both of his high-achieving daughters. I posed to him the question, "If Serena [not her real name] had a broken leg, do you think she should be required to run the 600 meter race for a major grade?" Obviously, he said no. "Why not?" I asked. "Shouldn't all students have to do the same things without any kind of modification?" He knew I had him, but he carried on. "It wouldn't be fair to make Serena run on a broken leg. In fact, it could even be harmful for her to run on it. Also, she would be academically penalized for something she could not control. That's just not fair. It's not right."

At that point, I brought it home. "Sean [not his real name], some students have academic broken legs. They didn't ask for them and they cannot solve the problem without time, energy, and help. That's why some students get instructional and assessment modifications, and sometimes special transportation, that every student does not get." At this point, he got it and voted appropriately. I was very proud of him and made sure to let him know it. Figure 8.3 expresses the importance of the equitable distribution and utilization of instructional resources.

The needs of every student must be looked at individually to determine the exact resources, instructional strategies, assessment mechanisms, and anything else they may need to have an equitable opportunity to enhance their learning success. Watch for questions that may be designed to determine if you have bias toward students with special needs or the legal issues regarding disabilities of any kind and if you have a clear understanding that whatever is necessary to meet student needs is what must happen. These concepts are important both on the test and, even more importantly, in your role as a superintendent. You must do both the legal and the right thing (001). Watch for questions that are checking to see if you know these things, and respond appropriately.

Figure 8.3   Equity of Instructional Resources

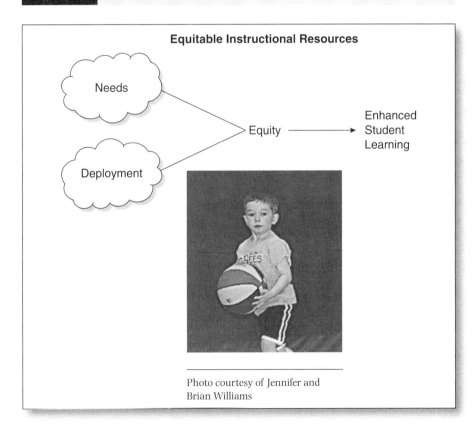

Equitable Instructional Resources

Needs

Deployment

Equity ⟶ Enhanced Student Learning

Photo courtesy of Jennifer and Brian Williams

- *Analyze the implications of various organizational factors (e.g., staffing patterns, class scheduling formats, school organizational structures, student discipline practices) for teaching and learning.*

This bullet is aligned with the sixth bullet in this competency as well as later in Domain III. The point they are trying to get you to understand and incorporate in your district is that *all* data (staffing patterns, class scheduling formats, school organizational structures, student discipline practices, etc.) must be analyzed for the purpose of improving teaching and learning. For example, say the district has been utilizing a set of specific bus routes for years. Time has gone on, housing patterns have changed, enrollments have increased, and the same bus routes are still in place. Based on the concepts presented in these domains and competencies, the Ideal Superintendent (i.e., you) would facilitate the development, articulation, implementation, and stewardship and evaluation (i.e., the 1–2–3–4 Plan) to determine if the current routes are effective or if they need to be modified. While bus routes may not seem like an academic issue, they are. If students, and particularly the youngest ones, have to catch a bus before the sun rises, there could be a problem. Likewise, if students are still waiting to get on a bus home after 4 p.m., that could also indicate a problem. Do routes need to be redrawn? Are more buses or drivers needed? What is the problem? How can it be resolved? *How can we do it better?*

Asking, "What is the problem?" cannot be answered appropriately without both short-term and long-term data. Therefore, as a proactive, informed decision-making superintendent, you will facilitate the analysis and implications of virtually everything taking place in the district in an ongoing manner. While you may be thinking that this is not a practical expectation, remember: This test is not designed to see if you know what practical is. It is designed to see if you know what ideal is. The Ideal Superintendent is assessing and improving everything all day, every day. He or she is constantly working to make everything better. Show the test that you know and are able to do exactly that. *You* are the Ideal Superintendent, and *you* are on top of everything.

- *Develop, implement, and evaluate change processes to improve student and adult learning and the climate for learning.*

Notice that "Develop, implement, and evaluate" are three pieces of the 1–2–3–4 Plan. The second component of articulation is assumed. How could anyone implement change without letting those involved and interested know what the change is, why it is important, what the goals are, and what is in it for them? Therefore, what this bullet is trying to communicate is the importance of developing a change process, using the 1–2–3–4 Plan, that is focused on improving student and adult learning (staff development, community education, etc.) as well as nurturing, supporting, and seeking to improve the district organizational climate. Whenever we ask, "How can we do it better?" the answers equate to a change process. The issues will always vary, but the need for ongoing, critical assessment and modifications based on the results will always be a change process. If something is assessed and determined to be effective with no changes recommended, this is not a failure of the process. It is evidence that the course of action is working. The process itself, the 1–2–3–4 Plan, has been the change. The conclusion and recommendation of no modifications being necessary at this time is then based on informed, data-driven facts rather than perceptions or comfort with a long-standing program or issue.

- *Ensure responsiveness to diverse sociological, linguistic, cultural, psychological, and other factors that may affect student development and learning and create an environment in which all students can learn.*

I just love this one. There are many reasons.

First, what it says is critically important not just to our schools, but also to our democratic and free society as a whole. Who would want leaders, whether they are educational leaders, business leaders, state and national leaders, or world leaders, who did not "ensure responsiveness to diverse . . ." virtually everything? How many times do we hear people complain that they are not being listened to, that their needs are not being met, and that, apparently, no one cares?

This bullet addresses all of these issues in an unbelievably wordy way. That is part of what I love about it. It says it all. Let's edit it a little bit to simplify what it is trying to communicate to us and to help you understand it. What if it said, "Ensure responsiveness to *all* (i.e., sociological, linguistic, cultural, psychological, and other) factors that may affect student development and learning"? Think about this. What kind of factor *wouldn't* impact student development and learning? September 11, 2001, sure did. Not having enough food at home, or money to pay the rent, or Daddy getting arrested, and so forth would also. So virtually anything or all things can and do impact student learning. Our role is to create an environment (i.e., culture and climate) in which every student can learn. We must address every need whether it is academic, social, cultural, health-related, or traumatic. If this sounds like it is the role of the superintendent to be all things to all people as in Figure 8.3, well, that pretty much sums it up. Again, you may be thinking that is not a reasonable expectation. Yet Figure 8.4 points out to us that highly effective superintendents do indeed serve as politicians, sociologists, economists, legal experts, and contemporary cultural anthropologists because they must understand and be able to address how each of these things impacts the larger contexts of the full

| **Figure 8.4** | Superintendents Serve as All Things to All People |

Highly Effective Superintendents
Serve as Politicians, Sociologists,
Economists, Legal Experts, and
Contemporary Cultural
Anthropologists

They

- understand the Larger Context.

- respond to the Larger Context.

- influence the Larger Context.

Photo courtesy of Ryan and Brittani Rollen

district. Let me remind you yet again: This test is not based on reasonable. It is based on ideal. Therefore, as a superintendent, you are seeking to create an ideal situation at all times. You are never tired, stressed, or weary. You just keep on making everything ideal all day long from now till forever. And that, folks, is the way we as educators will impact society and change the world one student, family, campus, and district at a time.

I love this bullet because it touches on virtually everything in life as something we should all be working together to improve. When we as educational leaders, working collaboratively with others, can impact society such that diverse sociological, linguistic, cultural, psychological, and any other factors are addressed within families, schools, churches, and communities, our world will indeed be a better place. Now, go do it. Do it in reality and, please, do it on the test.

GUESS MY FAVORITES

If Domain I was all about the vision, Domain II is about academic excellence and everything that must occur for all district students to be successful. There are many factors that impact student learning. Each of those must be addressed to meet student needs.

- Facilitate the development of a learning organization that encourages educational excellence, supports instructional improvement, and incorporates best practice.
- Ensure responsiveness to diverse sociological, linguistic, cultural, psychological, and other factors that may affect student development and learning and create an environment in which all students can learn.

IMPORTANT POINTS TO REMEMBER

- Everything related to instructional leadership and management should be focused on achieving the district vision.
- Advocate, nurture, and sustain (i.e., stewardship) district people and programs to develop or enhance the district culture.
- While 002 focused on ways to steward the district vision, this competency recommends the same strategies but varies its theme to curriculum, instruction, and staff development.
- Current research and best practices are essential to maximize district productivity.
- All decisions must be based on data.
- Data should be continually analyzed, synthesized, summarized, and used to make informed conclusions.
- High standards and expectations must be the norm rather than the exception.
- Be a good *steward* of the instructional program.
- Creating the culture means creating the conditions in which the vision can be attained.
- Always aim for excellence. Nothing else will do.
- Ensure that district programs meet the needs of all students and particularly those with special requirements.
- Guarantee resources are aligned with needs and are used appropriately.
- Be a positive change agent.
- Be responsive to everything that occurs to facilitate all students being able to maximize learning.
- *How can we do it better?*

Learner-Centered Human Resource Leadership and Management

DOMAIN II: Instructional Leadership

DOMAIN KEY CONCEPTS: Curriculum, Instruction, and Staff Development

COMPETENCY 007:

> *"The superintendent knows how to implement a staff evaluation and development system to improve the performance of all staff members and select appropriate models for supervision and staff development."*

Competency 007 is more than ensuring that the Professional Development and Assessment System (PDAS), which most Texas districts use, is implemented regularly and consistently. In fact, Texas law does not say that a district must use PDAS. It does specify exact criteria that the model must include. By the time the few districts that decided to create their own models did so, most instruments ended up looking remarkably like PDAS. Thus, today most Texas independent school districts use the PDAS model.

Whatever staff evaluation and development system is used, this competency does want it to be implemented with "with integrity, fairness, and in an ethical manner" (Competency 001) to improve the performance of every staff member. This includes paraprofessionals and other support staff. Obviously, they will not be assessed using PDAS, but their work should be consistently and fairly measured to see how it could be improved. Everything and everyone in the district, including you, should be supervised and assessed in an appropriate manner to their roles for the purpose of maximizing student performance. This is done through professional development that is aligned with personal and student needs. When we stop learning, we become stagnant. It is important for superintendents to be leaders of districts in every way including continuously looking for research-based ways to improve everyone's performance including their own.

THE SUPERINTENDENT KNOWS HOW TO . . .

- *Enhance teaching and learning by participating in quality professional development activities and studying current professional literature and research.*

As discussed in Competency 006, professional development is important for all members of the staff, including the superintendent. No organization can thrive long term without looking to the future, studying research, staying abreast of the current professional literature, reading, attending conferences and seminars, and so forth. Society and demographics will absolutely continue to change. In order for us to keep up with these changes, we must be constantly vigilant, "participating in quality professional development activities and studying current professional literature and research." *Read!* Make it a daily habit to read something relevant to the field, best practice, potential and new legislation, and so forth. *Participate!* Participate in as many professional development opportunities as you can while still keeping balance between your role as superintendent and your role in your family. Figure 9.1 shows the importance of quality professional development, including reading research and literature, to improve both teaching and learning. As long as we keep on doing what we have always done, we will keep on getting what we have always got. Are you satisfied with the status quo as it exists in education today? Me neither.

- *Develop, implement, and evaluate a comprehensive professional development plan to address identified areas of district, campus, or staff need.*

In Chapter 4, we covered the importance of the development, implementation, and evaluation of a district vision. We are revisiting this model again, but

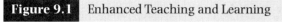

Figure 9.1   Enhanced Teaching and Learning

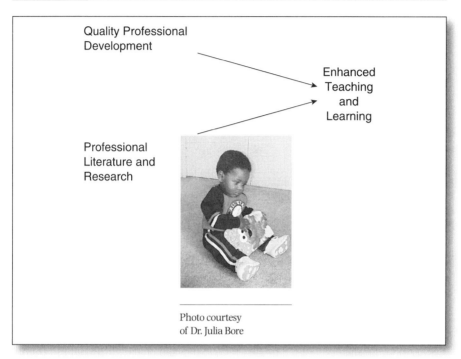

Photo courtesy
of Dr. Julia Bore

this time, it is in relation to a districtwide professional development plan. Both should be done after a complete analysis of multiple sources of student, campus, and district data, including district and campus Academic Excellence Indicator System (AEIS) Reports. These reports include student performance on the Texas Assessment of Academic Skills (TAKS) plus much data regarding student attendance, campus or district budgets, personnel, and programs. They are a primary source, but should not be the only source, of analyzing and summarizing student performance. These documents can tell you where areas of academic strength and weakness lie per subgroup, grade, content, and campus level as well as for the district itself. Based on these and other data, campus and district professional development plans should be created to meet the identified needs. These may vary campus to campus depending on the students involved, but there will be an overarching district plan in which needs are aligned to professional development activities. The basic underlying force should always be the needs of the students. Where the students need assistance, obviously the faculty does too. As shown in Figure 9.2, this is the way student data are used to determine teacher instructional needs, which subsequently should drive what and how professional development is determined, created, implemented, and evaluated.

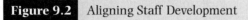

| **Figure 9.2** | Aligning Staff Development |

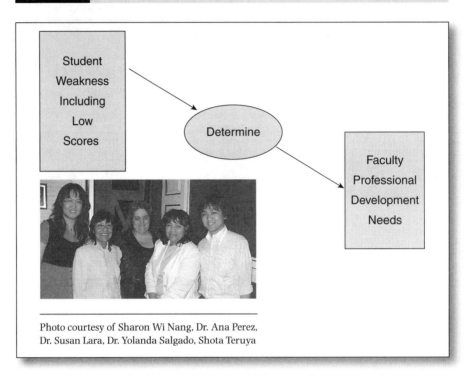

Photo courtesy of Sharon Wi Nang, Dr. Ana Perez,
Dr. Susan Lara, Dr. Yolanda Salgado, Shota Teruya

- *Facilitate the application of adult learning principles to all professional development activities, including the use of support and follow-up strategies to facilitate implementation.*

Adults are not children and should not be treated as such. As superintendents and other administrators work together to analyze data and prepare professional development activities, they should also include the people who will be impacted. These are usually the teachers. They will appreciate being treated as the professionals they are. Good teachers are acutely aware of their student needs and want to do the very best they can to address them. They will have good ideas. Not only will soliciting their input generate buy-in of the overall plan and its activities, it will also enhance the district culture and climate.

While teacher and other educator input plus data analysis are important, they are not the only things that should be utilized. Adult learning principles, including best practices; study styles; cultural, racial, and faith-based diversity issues; and emotional intelligence theories should all be included in making the activities interesting, engaging, relevant, and of immediate utilization to improve teaching and learning. Further, once a plan is collaboratively designed and implemented, things are not over. All activities should be evaluated and have follow-up. If something is not working, it should be changed. Do not keep doing something that is of no value. There is not enough time, plus it will really tick busy teachers off. If the horse is dead, get off. Get a new horse. Regroup. Analyze what went wrong, and fix it. If you do these things, you will be well on your way to being a good facilitator of data and adult learning principles for all professional development activities, including the use of support and follow-up strategies that facilitate their implementation, evaluation, and improvement.

- *Implement strategies to enhance professional capabilities at the district and campus level.*

What exactly are the professional capabilities of the staff on both the campus and district levels? What does this mean, and how do you do this? Synthesized data from teacher PDAS instruments are an excellent starting point. By disaggregating scores, you can have instructional strengths and weaknesses per teacher, campus, grade, and content levels determined. You will solicit input from both teachers and administrators involved to discern and utilize instructional strengths to develop compensations for weaknesses. This is the same manner in which the comprehensive professional development plan and activities are to be created. This time we are focusing on enhancing individual as well as campus and district professional capabilities. The pre- and post-PDAS conferences on the campus level between the teacher and the appraiser are a primary starting point for addressing potential areas of growth as well as congratulating jobs well done. Never forget to congratulate those who are working hard and doing their best. Sometimes their best isn't very good, but if you know it really is their best, that they are trying, and that they want to improve, your encouragement will go a long way to help them in their process of becoming more successful.

- *Work collaboratively with other district personnel to plan, implement, and evaluate professional growth programs.*

Earlier we discussed the importance of facilitating the application of adult learning principles to all professional development activities, including the use of support and follow-up strategies to facilitate implementation. We focused then, and continue to focus now, on the importance of working collaboratively with others in the district, including teachers, to brainstorm, contribute ideas, and discuss various ideas and methodologies that would be helpful in planning comprehensive professional development. Bringing this down to the individual teacher level, it continues to be important to do these same things in creating personal professional growth programs. Obviously, the appraiser is part of this process. If the appraiser is not the principal, then the principal should also be directly involved in conferencing with the teacher as well as facilitating the development and implementation of the growth program. It is always better for everyone to help a teacher grow than to terminate one. Our role as educators is to help all people succeed. This includes professional staff who, for whatever reasons, are not performing up to capacity.

- *Deliver effective presentations and facilitate learning for both small and large groups.*

As the superintendent, you should be the master teacher of the district. Just because you are not directly in a classroom leading instruction each day does not mean you are not teaching. Good leadership is good teaching. Therefore, you are both leading and teaching each day as you work with your staff, other district personnel, teachers, and the community. As such, you will be consistently called on to lead presentations before both large and small groups. Your communication skills, both verbal and nonverbal, will be very important as you do everything from leading administrative meetings to school board meetings in front of the public, campus meetings with teachers, or even presentations at community civic, social, religious, and philanthropic groups. If speaking in front of groups is something that makes you uncomfortable, begin practicing now. Talk in front of any group you can find, even if it is a Cub Scout group. Practice by pretending family members or good friends are your school board and convince them why something is expensive, but important. Ask them to play devil's advocate by asking you hard questions. Tell them to deliberately try to distract or stump you. They ought to love doing that. Start with really small groups and work your way up to larger ones as your confidence and comfort levels increase. Remember, sooner or later, you must interview with a school board so it can select you as superintendent. When interviewing with them, you are actually making a presentation. The subject of the presentation is selling yourself and the specific methods you will utilize to improve teaching and learning in their district. Later, after you have the job, you will be meeting with different groups, as described above, on almost a daily basis. Regardless of the topic, what you are really presenting, or selling to them, is how their district, where they pay taxes, will show improvement in teaching and learning. With all the media spotlights on the schools today, improving teaching and learning is a topic everyone is interested in. Education is one of the few areas of life that virtually all have an opinion about, and even consider themselves to be somewhat of experts, simply because once upon a time they went to school themselves. Your role is to always make every presentation you do be both informative and engaging. When you finish speaking, open the floor (or boardroom or whatever) to questions and be ready to answer. This is how you will build credibility both inside the district and in the school community itself. You want and need their full support to do the things you know are right for students. Doing presentations for anyone who will listen to you is an excellent way to build a support network from the ground level up.

- *Implement effective strategies for the recruitment, selection, induction, development, evaluation, and promotion of staff.*

With the shortage of degreed and certified educators across the nation, and in Texas in particular, there is a constant need to recruit, select, mentor, evaluate, and promote teachers, staff, and other administrators new to the district. There are particular shortages, even critical shortages, of educators for fields such as English as a second language (ESL), bilingual education, special education, and all areas of science and math. It is encouraging to note that there is an increase in the number of people with degrees in various fields who are choosing to return to a university or alternative preparation program to obtain teacher, or other, certifications. Goodness knows we need them. These people have already gone the traditional noneducation career route but, for various reasons, did not find it satisfying or meeting their needs. The truth is they want to impact society, to make it better, by teaching or leading a school. God bless them each and every one.

Your initial role is threefold:

- **Recruitment:** How do you find these people and get them interested in your district versus all the others who are recruiting as actively as you are?
- **Induction, Mentoring, Evaluation, and Retention:** Once you get them signed and teaching in your district, how do you properly orientate, support, and evaluate them personally and professionally so you can keep them and help them grow?
- **Promoting:** In what ways can you encourage and support existing staff to pursue additional certifications or advanced degrees so you can "grow your own" future leaders?

Having a really good salary structure helps, but it is not the whole answer. All of education is notoriously low paying. Few people go through all they must go through, including multiple TExES exams, to become certified as a get-rich-quick plan. That is not happening. People become educators because they enjoy working with young people and imparting knowledge, yet also because they want to be a part of something greater than themselves. Teaching and leading are perfect examples of this internal motivation.

There are no single-shot plans for the recruitment, induction, mentoring, evaluation, retention, or promoting of faculty or administrators. Research has shown many models to be successful in various ways, but none that are perfect. Many are expensive and virtually all are critically time-consuming. Each district must work collaboratively, in the same ways we have previously discussed, to develop plans that are workable for them and that meet their individual district's needs and uniqueness. The thing about this for you to remember when you are taking the TExES exam is to pick answers that show you know you are supposed to be actively recruiting, inducting, mentoring, evaluating, and seeking to retain staff instead of simply hoping that the sun will shine and all of this will happen with no apparent forethought and planning. The days of people graduating from college as teachers, then standing in lines to get teaching jobs are over with no signs at all of them coming back. Today we have to prove what is so wonderful about our districts so that an applicant will pick us as well as us picking them. Many large and rural districts start school every year with substitute teachers because they just can't get enough certified ones to take the jobs or because the position is in a high need content area and they cannot find anyone with the right credentials. Regrettably, some districts end up having to use these substitutes for the entire year. If you can come up with a perfect plan to encourage more people to become not just Warm Body Teachers with Pulses, but really wonderful, caring, student-centered educators, let me know. I will be delighted to help you market it. It will become our own way of giving something important back to the world through a cause that is greater than we are.

- *Develop and implement comprehensive staff evaluation models that include both formative and summative assessment and appraisal strategies.*

The vast majority of the public school districts in Texas utilize the Professional Development and Assessment System (PDAS) for the evaluation of teachers. The purpose of PDAS is to improve teaching performance. That is the reason the "Professional Development" portion of the PDAS title comes first. Districts that do not utilize the PDAS model must use one that still includes developing and implementing comprehensive (meaning for everyone) staff evaluation that includes both formative and summative assessment and appraisal strategies. There are two critical attributes of the evaluation model to address here:

- o **Formative Assessment and Appraisal Techniques:** Formative assessment takes place while you are *form*ing plans for the appraisal. It consists of a teacher conference regarding the class and subject to be seen, goals of the lesson, potential instructional and assessment strategies to be utilized, a review of the lesson plans, anything unique about students in the class, and anything else the appraiser or teacher would like to discuss.
- o **Summative Assessment and Appraisal Techniques:** A summative conference takes place after the appraisal has taken place when a *sum*mary discussion will occur. It is like a formative conference in reverse. The appraiser and teacher discuss what was seen during the lesson, its effectiveness, a critique of the instructional strategies, assessment, and active student engagement therein, and ways to potentially make it better in the future. Summative assessment is also where growth activities are discussed and planned. Regardless of how good any educators are, including you and me, we still can improve. Our model is based on the premise that all of us should and will be growing all the time.

Since the PDAS model is not required by law in Texas, it is unlikely, but not impossible, that it will be referred to by name on the TExES exam. Regardless of the question, remember that all of us can and should be growing, that teachers should have formative and summative assessments, that walk-through observations are good things, not bad things, and that growth plans are something we can all benefit from. They should not be used exclusively for the "bad" teachers, but for all of us. My wonderful, beloved, and respected mentor and friend, Dr. John Hoyle of Texas A&M University, always told me, "Elaine, there's a funny thing about people who set goals. They tend to reach them." John is right. Whether you are planning to pass the superintendent TExES exam, get a new job, write a book, or buy a new car, having goals with specific activities to be done to get you where you want to be and having a timeline for getting them done will help you reach your goals. Therefore, in our personal as well as our professional lives, having goals and growth plans are good things for us all.

- *Diagnose organizational health and morale and implement strategies and programs to provide ongoing assistance and support to personnel.*

In Domain I, we discussed the importance of the district culture, climate, and vision. Without them, no organization can maximize success. To have no vision is like being lost and refusing to ask directions. Organizational vision guides decision making from current status to where you want to be. The culture and climate of the organization, whether a school district, campus, or shoe store, set the tone for standards, values, and success. Without a rich culture and climate, no unit can reach full potential.

For these reasons, vision, culture, and climate also have a strong role to play in Competency 007 in regard to organizational health and morale. While Competency 002 addresses them from the perspective of the educational community, 007 concentrates on the standpoint of organizational and individual improvement.

As a superintendent, how will you seek to measure and enhance the district's health and morale? How will you work with others to go beyond the business end of leading a district to creating a common sense of mission and unity that goes beyond what is printed on letterhead? What kind of programs, or things, will you implement to encourage and support all teachers, administrators, and staff to help them in all they do? These issues, in essence, are an overarching framework of the strategies and programs you plan to accomplish through the district's comprehensive professional development plan. By collaborating closely with all stakeholders, asking the right questions, and creating a culture and climate of common vision, you will effectively diagnose the district's organizational health and morale while also implementing strategies and programs to provide ongoing assistance and support to your personnel.

GUESS MY FAVORITES

For superintendents to be credible in encouraging others to be lifelong learners, they must model this in their own professional development. It is also critical to constantly be assessing the district's organizational health and morale to maximize support, resources, and encouragement to teachers and other system employees. Therefore, my favorites for 007 are as follows:

- Enhance teaching and learning by participating in quality professional development activities and studying current professional literature and research.
- Diagnose organizational health and morale and implement strategies and programs to provide ongoing assistance and support to personnel.

IMPORTANT POINTS TO REMEMBER

- The reason for a staff development and evaluation system is to improve efficiency toward greater student learning.
- Be a role model of lifelong learning by participating in diverse forms of personal development.
- Encourage others to grow professionally by providing opportunities for them to participate in developmental activities.
- Continuously assess internal and external professional growth activities to make them better and more relevant to teacher and student needs.
- Align staff development with student needs.
- Be a good presenter and communicator.
- Utilize both formative and summative assessment strategies for the purpose of staff growth.

Learner-Centered Business and Technology of District Leadership and Management

DOMAIN III: Administrative Leadership

DOMAIN KEY CONCEPTS: Finance, Facilities, and Safety

COMPETENCY 008:

> *"The superintendent knows how to apply principles of effective leadership and management in relation to district budgeting, personnel, resource utilization, financial management, and technology use."*

We have now completed Domains I and II. Domain I focused on the superintendent's leadership skills in developing and enhancing the district culture, climate, and vision. Likewise, Domain II focused on the superintendent's role with the district curriculum, instruction, and staff development. Domain III now shifts its focus to the role of the superintendent with regard to district finance, facilities, and safety for students and staff. Domain III also adds the management skills set, which superintendents must incorporate to keep the organization financially stable. This includes ensuring that facilities are up to date, clean, efficient, and that everyone involved has a safe work and learning environment. So, in addition to being the steward of the district's culture, climate, vision, curriculum, instruction, and staff development, as superintendent you are also the CEO. This is where your skills in organizational oversight, efficiency, and effectiveness of all programs and issues truly become intertwined.

Competency 008 specifically addresses these leadership and management issues in relation to district budgeting, personnel, resource utilization, financial management, and technology use as described below:

- **Budget:** Is it collaboratively developed and aligned with student and employee needs to help achieve the district vision?
- **Personnel:** Do we have the right people in the right positions to maximize their own skills and to best benefit student learning? Do we have appropriate numbers of employees, rather than not enough or too many, for each district function?
- **Resource Utilization**: Are we being cost efficient by maximizing our human, financial, district, and community resources to best meet the district vision?
- **Financial Management:** Are we managing district funds in a prudent, ethical, and carefully audited manner?
- **Technology Use:** Do we have up-to-date technological resources to best meet district needs? Do we have safeguards to protect the confidentiality and efficacy of people and programs?

These are the things we will specifically discuss now.

THE SUPERINTENDENT KNOWS HOW TO . . .

- *Apply procedures for effective budget planning and management.*

There are three key words in this criterion. They are *effective*, *planning*, and *management*. The superintendent's role is to be chief facilitator of everything. For example, you may not be the district internal auditor, but it is still your responsibility to apply the appropriate organizational oversight to ensure the budget is planned, implemented, managed, and evaluated to optimize ethical, legal, and prudent utilization of every tax dollar. Few things will get you in trouble faster than if the public perceives, rightly or wrongly, that tax dollars are being wasted.

The steps in developing a budget are similar to those used in developing the district vision and anything else. As shown in Figure 10.1, effective budget planning and management must be strategic and aligned with targeted district (student) needs. These are consistently maintained to ensure ongoing assessment of effectiveness for future budget cycles. The

Figure 10.1   Strategic Budget Planning and Alignment

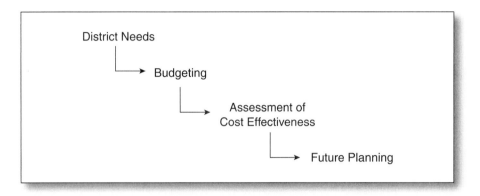

District Needs

Budgeting

Assessment of
Cost Effectiveness

Future Planning

process is continually repeated to ensure systematic district effectiveness and renewal.

In so doing, first you will collaborate, solicit, and facilitate others to identify prioritized needs in every area of the district, from teaching and learning to safe buses to facilities management. Look at the data to make rational decisions about where limited funding should go. As shown in Figure 10.2, collaborate with campuses, program directors, district and community planning committees, parents, citizen groups, and so forth to

Figure 10.2   Multiple Stakeholders Help Prioritize and Align District Resources With District Needs

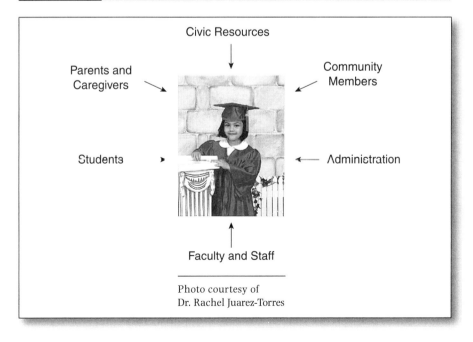

Civic Resources

Parents and
Caregivers

Community
Members

Students

Administration

Faculty and Staff

Photo courtesy of
Dr. Rachel Juarez-Torres

develop an understanding of the many district needs with limited state, federal, and local funding sources.

Superintendents rarely like to raise taxes if it is at all possible to avoid. Yet school districts are often handicapped by both state and federal "unfunded mandates," where policies, rules, and regulations are adopted but not paid for. Subsequently, they fall on the district's budget to address, which stretches tight dollars even further. For all these reasons, creating a prioritized budget to meet district needs and responsibilities is essential.

Every district has its own way of budget development. This test will stick to your understanding of budgets being created through collaboration with others, identified district needs, regulatory and statutory requirements, and alignment with the district vision, goals, and objectives. Districts will also have various procedures they use prior to adoption by the board. Final adoptions are precipitated when the state informs districts of the amounts of funding they will receive that year for various programs. These monies are determined by various formulas, thus the term *formula funding*. However, all districts must adopt both a budget and the tax rate necessary to sustain it by specified state dates. Usually these dates are set for late summer, whereas most districts begin their budget planning process for the following school year not long after Christmas. In order to solicit appropriate grassroots information, obtain and analyze data, and align funding with the district vision, goals, and objectives, much time is needed. Even when districts begin planning early and prudently, budget development and adoption is an important, in-depth, and time-consuming process.

Once a budget is adopted, the process is not over. Whether or not the district has a chief financial officer (CFO), all budgets must have a continuous process in place to ensure proper utilization of funds. Districts are required to have an external audit every year. Your goal is for that audit to go as smoothly, cleanly, and seamlessly as possible. For that to occur, appropriate mechanisms must be in place on a day-to-day basis to ensure fiscal responsibility. Each month, expenditure reports will be reported to the school board. Some boards are more "hands on" in going through these than others. Often, the smaller the district, the more intensely the board watches system finances. Ironically, the smaller the district, usually the less support staff you will have to address this very important issue. That means you could easily end up as the CFO as well as the CEO of your district.

Regardless, few things will get you in trouble faster than financial inaccuracies or even the perception of fraud or wastefulness, or a bad audit. Applying procedures for effective budget planning and management is a continuing process that goes on every day of the year. Guess who is ultimately responsible for it. You are. Conduct yourself accordingly.

- *Work collaboratively with stakeholders to develop district budgets.*

We discussed the importance of working collaboratively with stakeholders to develop district budgets. The importance of this process is reiterated by the work having its own criterion. Budgets must be built from the grassroots level up. All of the greater district community should have opportunities for input into budget development beyond the public hearings required by law. Input should be actively solicited via all forms of communication and media outlets. Campuses and programs themselves are critically important in this. Teachers especially want, need, and deserve to have a say in how much and for what purposes monies are allocated for their campuses. As we have discussed before, people support what they help create. If teachers and others have a thorough comprehension of the budget process as well as how the district receives funding (local, state, federal, grants, etc.), they can subsequently better understand where funding will go and why it will go there. Few educators ever feel there is enough money to go around. Outsiders may think too much money is being spent on education. Somewhere in between lies the truth. Again, your and your staff's communication skills are essential in creating this understanding and buy-in. The inclusion of and collaboration with others in the budget planning process is critical in the short- and long-term success of the district, so utilize these techniques wisely.

- *Facilitate effective account auditing and monitoring.*

Large districts will have entire departments of personnel whose education and experience lie in finance. Even in those districts, the superintendent is the one who will catch the flack and suffer the consequences if something goes wrong. Regardless of the issue, the buck stops with you. It is your job to ensure that all financial issues are audited and monitored in a systematic versus random manner. There should be specific procedures and checks and balances in place to prevent fraud, corruption, and just plain ineptitude in dealing with money. Superintendents can sometimes fall into the black hole of thinking everything is being done according to standard accounting practices, only to learn too late that is not true. Superintendents have even gone to jail for lack of prudence in financial oversight. Of course, I want you to pass this test. However, I also do not want to hear about you being arrested someday. Be very, very cautious in this area. The smaller the district, the more financial responsibility will fall on your shoulders. Do not let anything bad happen to the district . . . or to you. Guide your board to always hire the best external auditors they can afford. If the best firm costs more than a lesser quality firm, think carefully before making a decision. Sometimes things can be "pay me now, or pay me later." Audits of districts funds are not an area to skimp on.

- *Establish district procedures for accurate and effective purchasing and financial record keeping and reporting.*

There is an old saying that you must have a plan for anything you do. Then you must work the plan. This is true for everything from school district purchasing and financial record keeping and reporting to campaigning to become president of the United States. Every district will have established procedures in place to address record keeping and how purchasing is done. Most districts will have a purchasing director, many with multiple employees therein. But every district will have procedures in place.

You need to assess immediately upon employment whether the procedures that are currently in place are efficient and effective. Are they up to date, utilizing appropriate technology, and meeting all state requirements and district policies? If not, begin right away to solicit input into enhancing or improving them. This is an area that must be cutting edge. Immediately begin assessing the district procedures for accurate and effective purchasing and financial record keeping and reporting. If they barely exist or need improving, make this a top priority.

- *Acquire, allocate, and manage resources according to district vision and priorities, including obtaining and using funding from various sources.*

We discussed in the first criterion the importance of aligning the budget with the district vision, goals, and objectives. They are the reason the district exists, so they must be our first and foremost financial considerations. Neither district nor campus budgets should be sporadic. They also should not cater to different people's favorite programs or "sacred cows," that is, programs that have been in place forever regardless if they are most effectively and efficiently doing what they are supposed to do. Sometimes programs outlive their usefulness but are not ended because "That's the way we have always done it." Well, duh! Today's districts cannot afford any programs or projects that are not being regularly evaluated for efficiency and effectiveness in meeting district and campus goals. If there is a better and more cost-effective way to do something, it's time to make a change.

District funding comes from many different sources. Local school taxes are only one funding source. Most districts receive funds from the federal government, which are used for multiple things from free and reduced-priced meals to special education, reading, underserved populations and faculty development. Some districts have specific personnel whose primary role in their jobs is to seek, apply, and get grant funding from the government and anywhere else they can find it. There is always a need for more money. There are always programs and personnel that need to be supplemented or even initially developed. To have the funds to do these things, external funds are always being sought.

A large amount of district funding comes from the state each year. However, amounts will vary per year depending on the formula funding previously discussed, district enrollment, and wherever the Texas public school finance issues, lawsuits, and so forth are sitting with the courts and the legislature. For many years, Texas public school finance has been an ongoing volleyball game between them with each seeking to pass the buck back to the other. The losers each time are the districts and students. With neither the courts nor the legislature willing to make the hard decisions necessary to provide equitable public school funding, time continues to go by with districts always in flux, waiting for the next legislative session or court ruling. Regardless of the long-term outcome, your role as superintendent is to maximize the money you do acquire, allocate, and manage from any source to most effectively reach the district and campus vision, goals, and objectives based on collaborative input from as many stakeholders as possible.

- *Use district and staff evaluation data for personnel policy development and decision making.*

All districts in Texas are required to evaluate personnel for the primary purpose of increasing student learning. For teachers, the primary instrument used is the Professional Development and Assessment System (PDAS). Assessors are required by law to be trained and certified in Instructional Leadership Development (ILD), a model of curriculum, instruction, and assessment, as well as PDAS before they can appraise teachers. Both are based on best practices and are used for the purpose of improving teaching and learning. The PDAS system is not a "gotcha" system to get rid of under-performing teachers, but a tool to help all teachers grow to their own capacity as instructional leaders in classrooms. Data from PDAS evaluations should be utilized in triangulation with as many forms of student assessment as possible to align faculty and staff professional development with the needs of the students. For example, if students on a certain campus are scoring low in mathematical estimation skills on several forms of assessment, this is an indication that faculty, staff, and even administrator professional development is needed in helping them research, practice, and apply new or better techniques to best teach estimation. In this way, professional development decision making is data based upon the needs of the students.

All districts have policies in place in regard to personnel hiring, retention, and termination. You have two primary responsibilities:

- o **Evaluation of Existing Policies:** Are the policies that are currently in place timely, legal, and of the most benefit to the district? If not, begin a study and analysis process on how to best improve them to meet district priorities and to improve student performance.

Remember, everything you and the district do should be to improve student performance.

o **Application of Policies:** As long as a policy is in place, you must apply it consistently to all people. In addition to mismanagement of funds, another area that will get you in trouble quickly is to treat different people differently. Be consistent. If there is a policy that is inappropriate and needs correction, take it to the board and suggest changing it. Until then, use it for everyone and everything. There should be no double standards, no favorites, and absolutely no nepotism.

By doing these things, you will be using data to drive the district and staff evaluation for personnel policy development and prudent decision making.

- *Apply knowledge of certification requirements and standards.*

As you know, teacher and other educator certification requirements and standards have a tendency to change regularly. Part of this is due to keeping up with federal No Child Left Behind interpretations. Others could relate to Texas legislative or State Board for Educator Certification rules and regulations. Regardless, it is an important issue and one on which you do not wish to make any mistakes. After all, the education of students depends in large part on the quality of the teachers who are teaching them.

Most districts have a personnel director, or an entire personnel department, whose primary responsibility is putting the best and most qualified teachers in classrooms. These are the folks who address the basic issues of hiring, retaining, and dismissing professional as well as nonprofessional staff. It is of utmost importance that they stay on top of every issue; every caveat which addresses certification, progress toward certification, standards; and anything else that relates to staff being and doing their very best to create or convey a positive district, campus, and classroom culture and climate learning environment. Yet, while they are the ones who do this on a daily basis, you must still be an expert yourself. You are the one who is ultimately responsible for every district employee. If anything goes wrong, even if it is a school bus involved in an accident, guess who is going to hear about it. Yes, that's you. It is also you who briefs the board on multiple forms of personnel issues. You must know what you are talking about or they will not be a bit impressed. While you may not have it as your top priority to substitute as the personnel director for an extended absence, you still must be able to apply knowledge of certification requirements and standards at all times.

- *Apply knowledge of legal requirements associated with personnel management, including requirements relating to recruiting, screening, selecting, evaluating, disciplining, reassigning, and dismissing personnel.*

This criterion goes hand in hand with the one previous to it. Indeed, being able to apply your knowledge of all legal requirements that are associated with personnel management is critically important to the success of the district. Obviously, this is another top, shared responsibility with the personnel department. But you cannot pass this buck. It is too important. You also must stay on top of everything that relates to classrooms, teaching, and learning. This is why we are educators. It is why we have schools and school districts to begin with. You are the first face of the district. As such, not only must you be cognizant of all recruiting, screening, selecting, evaluating, disciplining, reassigning, and dismissing personnel issues, you must also be comfortable being able to articulate those issues inside and outside the district. Your knowledge and articulation of these subjects will do a lot to enhance the public perception of you as the educational leader of the community. You must know what is legal, what the best practices are, and what the prioritized needs of your district are and lead efforts to ensure the best personnel available is hired, developed, and retained to promote teaching and learning excellence. Remember, being the top administrator is more than meeting and greeting with the community. It is real work. This real work includes knowing what is going on all over the district, what is needed where, and being the facilitator of ensuring these things get done. Having the right people in place in every position is essential for achieving exactly that.

- *Manage one's own time and the time of others to maximize attainment of district goals.*

Upon first reading this criterion, you may think of it as an easy one. Everyone deals with time issues. There are not any specific laws for you to worry over in regard to time management. But let me tell you something: This one may be the hardest of all to actually accomplish.

In today's society, virtually all you meet, including educators, are busy, stressed, and tired. For many, these issues have gotten out of hand to the point of having a negative impact on their health. Drug and alcohol abuse are higher today than at any time in our past. Educators are certainly not immune to these things. In fact, with the continued pressure on all educators in regard to high-stakes testing, a case can be made that they are under more pressure and stress than ever before. All of us could name good teachers, counselors, diagnosticians, administrators, and so on who are retiring earlier than they really would like to because they are simply worn out from dealing with the stress of TAKS or other high-stakes tests.

Finding time for yourself under these circumstances, much less maximizing quality and relaxing time for others, can seem like only a dream. Believe me, this is one I totally understand. I'm with you!

But remember something we started this book with. This test is not based on reality. It is based on what the Ideal Superintendent would do to enhance or create the ideal district. In this ideal world, you would make time for rest for yourself. You would work with campuses to create ways to relieve stress for employees. One way is to include the employees themselves in this planning process. I cannot think of a single issue that would mean more to classroom teachers than to know that the superintendent cares enough about their well-being as humans as to solicit their input on ways the district can partner with them to make their lives better. Some ideas likely will not work. Some may be totally absurd. But others may be very good. There are many time management models and strategies available today. Empower others to research them, see what has worked in other educational settings, and create ideas and plans of what might work here. With a little creativity and willingness to get out of the status quo box of the ways we have always done things, we can make such an important difference in the lives of ourselves and others. Anything we do that helps others and ourselves become happier, healthier, and more at peace is a good thing. It will manifest itself in educator effectiveness inside classrooms resulting in, it is to be hoped, improved teaching and learning to reach district and campus goals.

Please do not blow off this criterion. It is so very, very important to you as well as to everyone around you. All of us, sooner or later, have times when we've done just about all we can do. Our bodies as well as our souls just cannot take on one more thing. Don't quit. Do not retire early. Take a few steps back to stop, to think and reflect, and to make some tough decisions about even good things you can give up to be able to be better at others. Protect yourself. Protect your spirit and your soul. Don't be afraid to sacrifice the important for the critical. You, the staff, and the district will all be better for it.

- *Develop and implement plans for using technology and information systems to enhance school district operations.*

Widespread utilization of technology is now an everyday occurrence. Even prekindergarteners are using it in class. Obviously, technology is equally critical all the way from the prekindergarten classroom to the superintendent's office. You must be a role model for the district and community in your personal utilization of it as well as your support for others to do likewise. This support must come in every way from the financial arena to incentives to verbal communication and encouragement to others.

As superintendent, you will be the ultimate person who is responsible for the development, implementation, assessment, and modification of strategic technology plans for the district. This responsibility must include all forms of information management systems to improve each facet of district operations. It will incorporate everything from attendance, discipline, Public Education Information Management System (PEIMS) data, scheduling, bus routes, all forms of maintenance, grades, students who are at risk and criteria, athletic schedules, and beyond. There is really very little data that cannot be better managed through the utilization of appropriate technology. Your job is not to devise the plans or procure the technology. It is to facilitate that all of it gets done, is continuously monitored, and is always the best the district can afford to maximize workplace effectiveness and efficiency.

- *Apply pertinent legal concepts, regulations, and codes.*

This one pretty much speaks for itself. Obviously, all of us as educators must keep the law and play by the rules. There is nothing that says you must agree with every law, regulation, and code, but you must support them. This is particularly true in public.

That is not to say you cannot dislike something and seek to change it. Just make sure you address potential change in a positive manner. No one wants a whiney superintendent. Change can be good, provided it is positive, well thought out, and systematic.

There will not necessarily be any lower level thinking skills "factual" test questions, which ask you to name a specific law or regulation. What you will encounter will be responses that are legal and others that are not. The way you will show your competency in applying pertinent legal concepts, regulations, and codes will be by utilizing higher level thinking skills, thinking things through, and selecting answers that do meet every standard. Therefore, you do not need to memorize your law books. You do need to understand current law so you will be able to apply it appropriately in answer selections.

GUESS MY FAVORITES

Here, we are in Domain III, but we are still focused on the district vision and how to maximize its attainment.

- Acquire, allocate, and manage resources according to district vision and priorities, including obtaining and using funding from various sources.
- Manage one's own time and the time of others to maximize attainment of district goals.

IMPORTANT POINTS TO REMEMBER

- Be a good manager as well as a good leader.
- Use student needs–based collaboration and alignment in preparing the district budget.
- Facilitate the utilization of effective monitoring and auditing of financial procedures.
- Analyze educator performance via the PDAS or other performance model based on student success as a dominant criterion.
- Ensure prudent and appropriate safeguards are in place for all financial issues.
- Utilize secure technology to enhance district operations and test it regularly.
- Be knowledgeable and able to apply all federal, state, and district policies and regulations regarding everything imaginable.
- Keep everything legal, moral, and ethical.
- Manage your time, or it will manage you.

11

Learner-Centered Support Systems and the Physical Plant

DOMAIN III: Administrative Leadership

DOMAIN KEY CONCEPTS: Finance, Facilities, and Safety

COMPETENCY 009:

> *"The superintendent knows how to apply principles of leadership and management to the district's physical plant and support systems to ensure a safe and effective learning environment."*

While writing this book, I spent time in beautiful, tiny, and marvelously quiet Winter Park, Colorado. I love to go to Winter Park. I thrive in the beauty of the solitude, of the Rocky Mountains, of the aspen and pine trees, of the sound of the wind coming through them, and particularly of the complete and total absence of human noise. All of this really works for me. Going there is like food for both my body and soul. I can walk in and feel my entire self relax.

While I was there this past year, a huge storm with tornados came through the northeast Colorado area. Interstate 25 was closed, entire communities were without power, and two semitrucks were overturned due to the extremely high winds and tornados that had ripped through the region.

During this time, several schools were placed in "lockdown." Parents were asked not to come get their children, and older students with cars were not allowed to leave campus in them. There was concern that everyone was safer where they were than on roads amid thunder, lightning, extremely strong winds, rain, and snow, all of which were often happening at the same time. All of these restrictions were in an effort to "ensure a safe and effective learning environment."

While we do not often have storms of this magnitude, sometimes they do happen. When they happen, we have to be absolutely positive that every campus and every facet of the district knows what to do, has practiced how to do it, and that a sense of calm and security is displayed in how the practiced procedures are carried out. In an effort to do this, Competency 009 primarily addresses two main issues:

- The district's physical plant and support systems
- Ensuring there is a safe and effective learning environment so teachers can teach and students can learn

Make sure you know and understand the terminology in this competency. The district's "physical plant" refers to the buildings and other structures. The "support systems" are all the other things that go into the smooth operation of a school district. They include everything from air conditioning and heating to energy management, maintenance, custodial work, and multiple district departments. All of them must be operating at peak efficiency, and all of them eventually come under your leadership and management. Someone else may be in charge of each department or endeavor, but sooner or later, the buck will stop with you. That means it is your job to stay on top of these issues even though they are not curricular or instructional. They are necessary to the efficient and timely operation of the district, which means that buck really does stop with you.

The TExES exam developers seem to love to play word games. They often come back to the same ideas repeatedly, but they use synonymous terms. For example, here in 009, they refer to a safe and effective "learning environment." What is another term we have discussed repeatedly that means the same thing as "learning environment"? Climate. Learning environment goes hand in hand with the district climate. So when they say you are expected to manage and lead a safe and effective learning environment, they are also saying that they want the climate (Competency 002) to be advocated, nurtured, and sustained (Competency 006) regardless of if it is in relation to the district vision (Domain I), to curriculum, instruction, and staff development (Domain III), or to district finances, facilities, and student safety.

THE SUPERINTENDENT KNOWS HOW TO . . .

- *Apply procedures for planning, funding, renovating, and constructing school facilities.*

District campuses and facilities are the primary impression many people have of the district itself. While good instruction and student learning can occur in poor buildings, they should not have to. Facilities are an important criterion when considering the importance a district places on the education of its students. While exercising financial prudence, superintendents, in conjunction with their school boards, should seek to provide the best possible places for teachers to teach, students to learn, co- and extracurricular activities to occur, and the community to support. While Domain I focused on the superintendent's role in facilitating the district culture, climate, and vision, and Domain II on curriculum, instruction, and staff professional development, here in Domain III, the emphasis has shifted to the facilities where these things occur and the financial and accounting responsibility necessary to ensure they happen in a prudent and transparent manner and that they are safe for all concerned. Therefore, as superintendent, you will lead the effort to ensure careful planning and needs assessments occur to evaluate the funding, renovating, and constructing of new school facilities. Just because a building is old does not mean it must be replaced. Age is not the primary criterion. Regardless of the age of any facility, the primary question is, are student needs being effectively met in this structure? If not, how can we make it better? Is it cost effective to renovate or to add onto an existing location? Are state standards being met? Can they be achieved through renovations? Or is it simply time to build a new campus? Has district growth exceeded capacity? These and many other individual district criteria must be addressed in a collaborative manner to ensure district facility needs are being appropriately addressed.

- *Implement strategies that enable the district's physical plant, equipment, and support systems to operate safely, efficiently, and effectively.*

Highly effective superintendents are good managers as well as excellent leaders. Figure 11.1 addresses this from the perspective of the superintendent being a good manager of the district as an organization, its operations, and its resources.

Figure 11.1	Successful Superintendents Are Managers and Leaders

Highly Successful
Superintendents Are Good
Managers as Well as Leaders

- *They manage and lead
  district*
  - Organization
  - Operations
  - Resources

Photo courtesy of Shota Teruya and Dr. Elaine Wilmore

Age and size are only initial issues in assessing the district's physical plant, equipment, and support systems. For you to be successful on this test, you first must know and understand exactly what the terminology means. What are the physical plant, equipment, and support systems? The physical plant does not mean district landscaping. The physical plant is a collective term used to address all district buildings and structures. Schools are, obviously, part of the district's physical plant. But so are all auxiliary structures, from the central administration building to maintenance facilities, athletic fields, fine arts arenas, the bus barn, and so forth. If it belongs to the district, it is part of the physical plant. That means that on the test you must be watching for questions that address needs in every area. Watch for questions and potential responses that address facilities that may go beyond classroom space. Do not assume that since direct learning is not taking place in a bus barn that that response is wrong. Very few districts can operate efficiently, effectively, and safely without buses. On the other hand, never assume that because a potential response does address a less likely facility that it is the correct answer. Always look for the best response to exactly what the question is addressing. Underline key words in the question. This will help you remain focused on the specific response necessary to get the question correct.

Continue in this way with the district's equipment (i.e., things the district owns) and support systems (i.e., everything and everyone that provides support in helping students learn even in the slightest manner). Equipment ranges from computers to copy machines to software to basketball backboards to curriculum to texts to paper and pencils. Support systems range from proper heating and cooling systems to student services such as speech therapy, guidance, and counseling. Together, they address every issue that serves to enhance student learning. As superintendent, you are the primary overseer to ensure teachers have everything they need to meet their campus and district visions, goals, and objectives in a financially prudent, effective, efficient, and safe manner. Watch for questions and responses written to see if you know the buck does, indeed, stop with you. Teachers, and all educators, must have the physical plant, equipment, and support systems they need to maximize student learning in a safe, effective, and efficient manner. It is your job, in reality as well as on the TExES exam, to see that they have it.

- *Apply strategies for ensuring the safety of students and personnel and for addressing emergencies and security concerns.*

Student and educator safety and security are on everyone's minds now more than ever. Times are over when the largest safety concerns were weather related, having appropriate heat in the winter, and regular fire drills to keep the fire marshal happy. Schools today face everything from complex student custody issues to deranged people with bombs to students (or others) with guns who seek to kill innocents and often themselves. Because of these issues, and others, every district and campus must have an emergency and crisis management plan that all participants are truly familiar with and have practiced, so that they know exactly what to do if an emergency arises. There is just no way anymore to leave emergency plans to chance. They must be planned for, evaluated, and consistently massaged and edited to keep up with everchanging community, national, and global society changes. Remember, it is not enough to have a plan. All stakeholders must be thoroughly familiar with it. They must have repeatedly practiced it. Everyone must know exactly what to do if a true emergency ever actually does arise. This test will not ask you technicalities of a model state emergency or crisis management plan. They will differ from district to district depending on multiple community variables. What you will be tested on is your firm awareness that all districts and campuses must have an adopted emergency and crisis management plan that is well articulated and practiced and that in the awful event that it ever has to be truly utilized, it will unfold in a flawless manner. The goal, as always, is for the emergency and crisis management plan to operate smoothly in an efficient, effective, and safe manner for the protection of everyone.

- *Develop and implement procedures for crisis planning and for responding to crises.*

This concept is simply putting into words what we have been discussing throughout Competency 009. Obviously all districts must develop and implement procedures or strategies for planning for and responding to a crisis. I would have made this the first bullet because it is the "big umbrella" under which all the rest of the bullets fall. Regardless of where it is placed, this is one of the most important concepts to be presented in Competency 009. As superintendent, you must make sure your district has developed and implemented solid crisis management plans and that a system is in place for their practice and evaluation. Things change, people change, society changes. A plan developed in the same district five years ago likely needs modifications today. Please note this bullet specifically says, "Develop *and* implement." Both are important. Do not just make sure a plan has been developed. Assess it. Make sure it is practiced. Modify it as needed. All of these are parts of implementing it efficiently and effectively. Having an unpracticed and unassessed plan for anything sitting on a shelf or being stored in a computer isn't doing anyone any good. Knowing there is a plan in policy somewhere won't do a campus a bit of good when someone shows up with plans to blow up the place. It's too late to start thinking about what it might say then. Develop, implement, assess, and modify now. Do not wait. Do not procrastinate. There is nothing entrusted to us that is more important than the safety of our students and employees. While other people do have responsibilities in this area, it is ultimately the superintendent who must ensure the district has developed and implemented procedures for crisis planning and for responding to crises. The buck really does stop here.

- *Apply procedures for ensuring the effective operation and maintenance of district facilities.*

Some of the most overlooked and underappreciated groups of people in education today are those in charge of the operation and maintenance of district facilities. Each campus will have a staff charged with keeping them clean. Each campus will have a lead or top custodian. Take care of these people! They have usually been with the district or the campus for a long time. They have keys to the buildings, know the history of both the custodial and the maintenance operations, and they know where the bodies are buried. While most districts have separate maintenance and custodial departments and staffs, the two teams usually work in an interactive manner. This necessitates good communication between them on both the district and campus levels. Thus, there should be procedures and routines that are followed in a systematic manner to ensure facilities are clean, safe, effective, and efficient. Policies and roles should be clearly defined and understood by all stakeholders including campus principals. Without each person, unit, and department understanding their purpose and means in helping the campus and district achieve its mission, chaos and hurt feelings can easily occur. In reality and on the TExES exam, make sure you address in every way possible that procedures for ensuring the effective operation and maintenance of district facilities are consistently applied at all times.

- *Implement appropriate, effective procedures in relation to district trans-portation services, food services, health services, and other services.*

One night a fire started in the cafeteria of an elementary school in East Texas. The fire was put out rapidly with little damage beyond the cafeteria. School was allowed to go on the next day without interruption. Unfortunately, the cafeteria did not fare so well. It was out of commission for some time. The district rushed to address the situation in—you guessed it— a safe, effective, and efficient manner. However, on the first morning after the fire occurred, the top question was, "How can we serve lunch today?"

The answer was McDonald's, of course. The students were thrilled to have McDonald's lunches, with milk, delivered to their classrooms. They considered the whole thing quite a lark. The cafeteria manager did not. Thankfully, other strategies were put into place to provide a nutritious breakfast and lunch to the students while the cafeteria was being renovated. Yet this true story certainly focused community attention on the importance of all aux-iliary services, particularly those involving food and transportation, on the operation of a district. Even though this fire occurred when no one was pre-sent or hurt, it still constituted a crisis for the campus. It is still of top impor-tance to address how to feed hundreds of children the very next day when a tornado destroys a building, when a roof collapses, or anything else. In other words, all emergencies do not necessarily involve weapons. Everything must be planned for in a positive and proactive manner while you are always hoping there is never a need to implement any of it. These are the things the TExES exam will want you to know. Remember, a shouting irate parent is indeed a crisis for someone. A suddenly out-of-control classroom is definitely a crisis to the teacher in charge. These things may not seem to rate on the same scale as an explosion at a chemical plant located next to a school. But they are still emergencies in their own right, particularly at the time they are happening. What are you as superintendent going to do to ensure plans are in place to address virtually any situation that could arise? How will you make sure there are appropriate and effective procedures in place for every facet of the district from transportation and food services to health and any other service? You are the Top Dog. While you may, or may not, be the one out on campuses training others in emergency management strategies, it is definitely your role to see that these things are being done. Your job is to ensure the district has appropriate plans, practices them, and is ready to work the plans if the need arises.

- *Apply pertinent legal concepts, regulations, and codes.*

The key word in this last concept is *apply*. When we consider Bloom's taxonomy, *apply* is a higher level thinking skill than simply knowing about something. Therefore, being able to apply or utilize all legal ideas, rules, and policies that are relevant to the district at large or any program therein is an essential skill to being a successful and valuable superintendent. Don't just know about legal concepts, regulations, and codes. Take time to consider, analyze, and understand what they represent so you can apply them in the daily efficient and legal operations of the district.

GUESS MY FAVORITES

Domain III focuses on the district finances, facilities, and the safety of its students. As such, the superintendent must manage the district's finances and facilities in such a way that everything possible, including crisis management, is done to protect the safety of students and staff.

- Implement strategies that enable the district's physical plant, equipment, and support systems to operate safely, efficiently, and effectively.
- Apply strategies for ensuring the safety of students and personnel and for addressing emergencies and security concerns.

IMPORTANT POINTS TO REMEMBER

- Global organizational attentiveness is critical to ensure everyone and everything is operating as it should.
- Manage the district buildings and support systems in a safe, effective, and efficient manner.
- Take care of district buildings and finances in a prudent manner.
- Be knowledgeable about facilities bond procurement.
- Develop, implement, practice, evaluate, and regularly update a relevant and timely emergency and crisis management plan.
- Be knowledgeable about district special programs including transportation, food services, health services, and other services.
- Ensure you are aware of, understand, and lead the district to implement appropriate and up-to-date legal concepts, regulations, and codes.
- The buck stops with you. Be aware. Keep your eyes open. Make sure everything is done right.

Learner-Centered Organizational Leadership and Management

DOMAIN III: ADMINISTRATIVE LEADERSHIP

DOMAIN KEY CONCEPTS: Finance, Facilities, and Safety

COMPETENCY 010:

> *"The superintendent knows how to apply organizational, decision-making, and problem-solving skills to facilitate positive change in varied contexts."*

Outside of ethics (Competency 001), few areas can get a superintendent in hot water quicker than having poor organizational, decision-making, and problem-solving skills. How many superintendents today lament one decision, which they truly thought was a good one, has come back to haunt them over and over through the years? Probably every superintendent has decisions that come up weekly that they wish they could take back or redo. So be careful with this competency. Do not write it off as the common-sense stuff. Some say there is an uncommon lack of common sense in district leadership today. I do not want that to be said of you. Therefore, collaborate, take the time, and utilize the appropriate resources to make good decisions, to solve problems in an ethical and legal manner (Competency 001), and to always be looking at moving the district forward through positive change in each context you encounter every day. Remember, sometimes it is the little decisions, more so than the large ones, that come back to bite you. People tend to take more time making decisions on big things than little things. Yet it is the little things that can add up to get us. In order to be the best superintendent your district has ever had, you must be cautious in how you apply organizational, decision-making, and problem-solving skills to facilitate positive change in varied, or different, contexts.

THE SUPERINTENDENT KNOWS HOW TO . . .

- *Implement appropriate management techniques and group process skills to define roles, assign functions, delegate effectively, and determine accountability for goal attainment.*

Knowing how to get groups of people to work well effectively takes more than skill. It is an art. All people bring their own talents and gifts to the group. Getting them to use those talents toward a collective vision or goal takes great effort. Yet that is exactly what successful superintendents do. They are like great symphony leaders who orchestrate exactly what each person or group is to do as well as when and how they do it. When it all comes together perfectly and everyone fulfills their own roles and functions, a complex yet melodic masterpiece is achieved. When individuals or groups do their own thing in their own way at their own time, all you get is noise.

We've had enough noise in our schools. It's time for the symphony. Therefore, the superintendent as symphonic conductor defines the role of each entity, assigns the functions, or things to be achieved by that group, delegates appropriate things to appropriate people and groups, and sets specific, targeted measures by which every single thing assigned will be assessed or held accountable. Every entity thus will have a clear understanding of what it are supposed to do, how it are supposed to do it, by when it should be accomplished, and how its work will be evaluated. People then have ownership in both the endeavor and their role in it. Their function is but a single melodic line, which, with those of others, will come together for the district to produce the best symphony ever. We've had enough noise from everyone doing their own thing. It's time to make beautiful music . . . together.

- *Implement processes for gathering, analyzing, and using data for informed decision making.*

The only way to make an intelligent and informed decision is to do it based on appropriate data and facts. We all know or have worked with those who have preconceived notions of the way things should be and what should be done. They are the same people whose attitude reeks of

"Don't mess me up with the facts. My mind is already made up." This is exactly why attorneys get to interview prospective jurors before a trial. They are looking for bias. If they can establish a potential juror has bias for or against a certain position or person, they work to get that potential juror eliminated. There is no place for bias in the courtroom. There is also no place for bias in school leadership informed decision making. Not only is it wrong, it's frankly downright dumb. We don't have time for dumb decisions any more than we have time for noise. We need cold hard facts. We must work with and lead others to disaggregate student test scores to determine individual as well as subgroup, campus, and district strengths and weaknesses. When a weakness is identified, specific collaborative plans must be made on how it will be improved. Hoping scores will be better next year gets no one anywhere. Getting down to the nitty-gritty of exactly where we are determines where we need to be. Every campus and district, led by the superintendent, must identify a model for gathering, analyzing, and using data for making informed decisions. Each district's model may vary. The important thing for you to remember in regard to this concept is that there must be a model, there must be specific, articulated, and clearly understood tools, strategies, and mechanisms in place by which data can be collected so decisions can be based on facts instead of perceptions. This takes the emotion out of tough decisions. The facts are what they are. Look at all the data in totality, get the big picture of what they say and indicate, and make informed decisions accordingly.

- *Frame, analyze, and resolve problems using appropriate problem-solving techniques and decision-making skills.*

Once a model, or template, is in place for gathering, analyzing, and using data for informed decision making, the next step is to determine how data can also be used to frame, analyze, and resolve problems. These issues are not limited to improving standardized test scores. Having and using appropriate problem-solving techniques and decision-making skills is necessary in addressing all educational as well as personal life conflicts, confusions, and resolutions. Getting people with opposite opinions to come to consensus is important in life and absolutely essential in district leadership. As superintendent you must be able to negotiate change based on data with groups as diverse as teachers, the school board, and the community. Superintendents who are not able to communicate well and wisely to facilitate conflict resolution and informed decision making can too often find themselves and their ideas misunderstood. Left unchecked over time, this can lead to unpleasant decisions being made at the ballot box when school board member elections are held. Different successful superintendents, as well as leaders of other organizations, must find the right tools that work for them. There is no perfect one-size-fits-all problem-solving technique that works for everyone. If there were, we would all be using it and the world would have no more conflict. Terrorism would end, the economy would blossom, and we would all stand around smiling and singing "Kum Ba Yah." Thus far, that's not happening. Each of us must find our own way of bringing different perspectives together, of finding common ground among people with strongly different views and opinions, and seeking together to create a common vision and strategies to achieve it. Yes, there are instances where this is very time consuming. Rarely does achieving a common vision come without obstacles. Yet true leaders have perseverance, courage, and persistence. They maintain a positive attitude and always keep conversations, discourse, and research focused on what is best for this district's unique set of students at this moment in time. Things may be different in the future. But for right now, this is our circumstance. Together, we must address it. How can we *best* and most *expeditiously* do that together? Involve stakeholders in answering these questions. Then go forward, and achieve greatness.

- *Use strategies for working with others, including the board of trustees, to promote collaborative decision making and problem solving, facilitate team building, and develop consensus.*

This one is actually very similar to the ones before it but with a different twist by this time including the board of trustees. Everything we have previously said still holds true here. We must still work to achieve a common vision by focusing on identifying and utilizing the things we can agree upon, even if there aren't very many of them. It is a starting point. Solicit collaborative input and feedback from all entities, particularly teachers and the school board itself during the development of plans on any issue. Collect multiple forms of assessment and other data that can be used to help formulate ideas for problem solving and informed decision making. Encourage people to keep open minds and not jump to conclusions based on perceptions or no data at all. Work with the school board and other administrators on various forms of team building, such as those offered through the Texas Association of School Administrators, the Texas Association of School Boards, and all of the Education Region Service Centers. Attending and actively participating in Team of 8 training with the board of trustees is an important tool that should be performed annually and as soon as possible after each election. Getting everyone working from the same perspective, understanding what needs to be done, obstacles involved, resources needed, and collaboratively seeking and valuing input from as many people as possible are all necessary to promote collaborative decision making and problem solving, facilitate team building, and develop consensus. Without these things, we are back to the noise we discussed earlier that we do not want. We are still wanting that beautiful yet complex symphony, which can be created when everyone displays a good attitude, positive work ethic, is open-minded to the thoughts and opinions of others, looks at data versus perceptions in making informed decisions, and seeks to works well with others.

- *Encourage and facilitate positive change, enlist support for change, and overcome obstacles to change in varied educational contexts.*

My greatly respected mentor and friend, Dr. John Hoyle of Texas A&M University, has said that although a lot of people say they want change, the only ones who really like change are wet babies. As usual, he has a point. Most educators like to think of themselves as progressive thinkers who are willing to do whatever is necessary to facilitate positive change, that is, increased student learning performance. Yet, because we are human, we all have our comfort zones. We all have ways we have done things in the past that have worked for us. Yet society today is not what it was in the past. Society is changing. Students are changing. And we must change with them. Our comfort zones are not the issue. Helping students maximize their learning, helping them reach for their own stars, assisting them with identifying and reaching their personal goals are all things that require us to get out of our previously successful boxes, look to the research, and try new curriculums and instructional methodologies. These are all ways we can model for others the importance of positive change. Remember, as long as we keep on doing what we have always done, we will keep on getting what we have always got. That is not good enough. We must do better. As superintendent, you must light the path for others to follow in inspiring and generating positive change for the benefit of individual students, campuses, the district, and society as a whole.

- *Apply skills for monitoring and evaluating change and making needed adjustments to achieve goals.*

If I have said it once, I have said it a thousand times. The number one question for each of us in life and in leadership should be, "How can we do it better?" What the "it" is, is irrelevant. It could be improving test scores, passing an important bond issue, hiring the best educators, winning the state championship in basket weaving, or improving the quality and quantity of our family time, losing weight, setting fitness goals, or enhancing our spiritual lives in whatever manner works for us; there is always room for improvement. We continue this paradigm by further asking, "Are there more effective and cost-efficient ways we can improve results?" Continually asking ourselves how to do everything in our lives better is such a realistic way to identify areas that need improvement as well as ways to actually get it done. Worrying and fretting never improved anything. Creating a plan with specific things to accomplish and a timeline by which to do them will improve virtually anything.

The next important step to remember is that this process must be continuous. Just because you improve one area does not mean you are through with it. We are never through. Until our districts and our personal lives are absolutely 100% perfect, we are not done yet. Since no one has invited me yet to come visit their *perfect* district, I'm assuming you are not finished with your quest toward perfection either. None of us are. None of us will be either until we start asking how we can improve every facet of our district and our lives 100% of the time without ceasing. Only then will we really be able to say we are soliciting, monitoring, and evaluating change and making the necessary modifications to make things better in how we are doing everything in our personal and professional lives. Only that will lead us and our districts to achieve our goals, improve targeted issues, and feel more professionally and personally fulfilled. Keeping on doing the same things in the same ways over and over is not going to get us where we want to be. Every day, in every facet of our lives, we must continually be asking ourselves how we can make everything, including ourselves, better.

- *Analyze and manage internal and external political systems to benefit the educational organization.*

If there is one thing we all can count on, it is that there will always be those who seek to help public education succeed and those who seek to bring us down. Some do it because they think they are doing the right thing. Others seek to create havoc on the schools simply due to attention-seeking behavior, mental illness, or having too much time on their hands. Wouldn't it be nice if we could turn all of the naysayers into passionate supporters of quality educations for all children regardless of their circumstances? It's a nice thing to think about, but how can we accomplish it?

Individuals and groups outside the educational arena, including the legislature, policy groups, professional organizations, and so forth are external political systems. Others that may be present are employees or others directly involved with the district; these are internal political systems. It is illegal for Texas teachers to unionize or strike. Yet some teacher "associations" are activist in nature. That is not necessarily a bad thing. It can, and often is, a good thing. Improved salaries, budgets, teaching conditions, and class size limits are just some of the benefits of both internal and external political systems. Having a student performance accountability measure is also a good thing. It becomes bad when too much emphasis is placed on a single test or measure and excludes other venues. Yet all of these are results of internal or external political systems. As superintendent, you are a classic example of no man being an island. You must become actively engaged in outreach to various diverse groups ranging from local civic clubs and businesses to the legislature. This can be done, at a minimum, through your membership and support of the Texas Association of School Administrators and other professional organizations. Your involvement can also extend to other entities, such as the Texas Equity Center, that seek to influence policy decisions and legislation. All superintendents must find their own ways to analyze and manage internal and external political systems to benefit the educational organization. Exactly how you choose to become actively engaged is a personal decision based on your time, interests, and comfort level. The real issues are that you are involved, that you solicit others to be involved, and that you are a walking, talking, active spokesperson for the importance of a free and appropriate education for all students regardless of any other factors.

GUESS MY FAVORITES

It is appropriate that this last competency, 010, focuses not just on goal attainment for today but also on encouraging and facilitating positive change for the future. The future is what everything we do in a free and democratic society is all about. It is nice that we close our competencies looking to encourage exactly that.

- Implement appropriate management techniques and group process skills to define roles, assign functions, delegate effectively, and determine accountability for goal attainment.
- Encourage and facilitate positive change, enlist support for change, and overcome obstacles to change in varied educational contexts.

IMPORTANT POINTS TO REMEMBER

- How can we make it better?
- Create consensus, problem solving, and conflict resolution by identifying common ground through tying everything to the collaboratively developed district vision and mission and data-driven decision making.
- Be a positive change agent.
- Never settle for the status quo.
- Have an accountability system whereby everything that is done gets assessed because everything assessed gets done.

- Ensure all involved people have clear definitions of their roles, functions, responsibilities, assessment mechanisms, and timelines.
- Make decisions based on data and research rather than perceptions or bias.
- Model and encourage collaboration for yourself, the board of trustees, and others.
- Do not take no for an answer just because something is a new idea, difficult to implement, or outside someone's comfort zone. Nurture and support others to participate in creative collaboration and brainstorming of better ways to do existing things.
- Monitor the change process. Stay on it 100% of the time.
- Be cognizant of managing internal and external political forces that can impact the district. This includes just about everything, so be alert to everything taking place around you that can, or could, impact your district.

SECTION III

The Real Deal

Practical Application

Data Analysis

How Do I Read All Those Reports?

DATA ANALYSIS SIMPLIFIED

Being able to analyze data is critical to your success as a superintendent and in passing either of the administrative TExES exams (superintendent or principal). Yet data analysis remains one of the things that tends to really frighten test takers. It should not. There are some basic tools to utilize that will help you get a profile of the data. Remember, the TExES exam is built around knowledge and skills that an *entry-level* superintendent should have. You do not need to know how to disaggregate data for a multivariate statistical doctoral dissertation to pass this test.

HOW TO READ AND INTERPRET STANDARDIZED TEST SCORES

There is no guarantee that you will have a decision set, or any other data to analyze and apply, that is built on standardized tests, their results, or their implications. However, there is also no guarantee that you will *not* either. Some people make a big mistake. They turn the page in their test booklet, see all those graphs, and think, "Here come those awful standardized tests," or, "Oh, dear. I really do not like math." Their first response is to panic.

But not you. You are not going to panic. You know that when anxiety goes up, productivity goes down. You do not want your productivity to go down. After all, how can you be calm, cool, collected, confident, and almost downright cocky if you are panicking? So, do not panic. Take a deep breath, blow it out slowly, and do what I tell you.

Read the prompt for the decision set or data analysis slowly for comprehension. It will lay the groundwork of what the questions will be about. It will give you the "feel" of what the test developers are looking for. There is never anything to panic over in the prompt. All the prompt does is to set you up. So read it and see what you are dealing with. Underline key words. Get the feel of the district or campus you will be analyzing.

Once you have done that, look at the charts or graphs provided. Think "big picture." At this point, you are *only* interested in the big picture. Standardized tests in these scenarios are usually achievement tests. They have been around longer than the Texas Assessment of Knowledge and Skills (TAKS) and are something virtually every district in the nation either is, or has been, dealing with. You need to know how to analyze, interpret, and utilize them to increase district student performance. These data will provide the parameters to tell you where your district's strengths and weaknesses are. They are crucial for strategic short- and long-term planning.

Look at each chart or graph individually. What are these data about? Identify it. What subject is the data referring to? Identify it also. Keep breathing slowly, deeply, and confidently. Frankly, you do not *care* what grade or subject it is, except to be prepared for whatever questions may, or may not, be coming your way. Do not think, "Oh, my goodness! These are math scores! I hate math, and I doubly hate math scores!" Do not go there. It will not make one bit of difference if the scores are math, reading, or science, or anything else. Scores are scores. The real question is what are you going to do with them? How are you going to lead and facilitate others to use them to make informed decisions that will impact the district vision, curriculum, and instruction? These are the important issues that the TExES exam will want to know that you know how to do.

Next, if you have a chart, look across the top and down the left side to see what your headings are. The headings will provide you with the categories of content that have been tested as well as the rating scales used.

Read the concepts the students have been tested on. They likely will be grouped in broad categories. This will provide you the basic overview of what was tested. This helps constitute the big picture that you want to have before you start to read the questions within the decision set. Look next at the rating scales to see how they are categorized.

At this point, you will make some obvious conclusions ranging from "This grade, content area, campus, or district did pretty well" to "This is horrible. I need to be in charge of this district to turn it around!" You may notice some particular areas where the grade, content area, campus, or district did very well, or some areas where they did particularly bad . . . which is a polite way of saying they stunk. More likely, the majority of their scores will be somewhere in between.

Stop here and listen to me. Do not play The What If? Game. Do not try to be psychic with the data by thinking, "What if they ask me something I don't know? What else can I conclude from these data? What *could* they ask me? Oh, my goodness. I do not even know what these concepts stand for! What if they ask me something I am clueless about?" While you are doing that, two things are happening:

- While you are playing The What If? Game of, "What if they ask me this or what if they ask me that?" your anxiety level is going up. We all know by now what happens when your anxiety level goes up. We do not want that. Definitely not! We do not want your anxiety level so off the scale as evidenced by regular huge sighs that people around you think you are having Prozac withdrawal. Leave The What If? Game alone. I will give you plenty of *productive* games—techniques to help you in the next chapter. Right now, just identify the broad categories, and move on. Do *not* try to read the minds of the test developers. After all, they got paid for developing the test. You did not. Your job is to pass it.
- The clock is ticking. You have plenty of time to take and pass this test. However, it makes no sense to waste the time you have. There is no reason for you to sit there, staring at all that data while playing The What If? Game. You do not want to *wonder.* You want to *know.* Thus, while you are wondering what they *might* ask you, the clock is ticking away your precious minutes. No, no, no! You are not going there. Turn the page. Go see what they *are* asking rather than fretting over *What If?* It is a better utilization of your limited time, keeps you on track and focused, and keeps you working *with* the clock rather than against it.

Remember, in your initial view of the data, all you want to do is get the essential part of what it is presenting, such as grade, subject, basic concepts tested, and an overview of how the district, grade, content area or campus performed.

Next, turn the page, and get started on the actual questions. This test is a mind game. Do not let it psych you out. Beat it at its own game. Keep reading, answering, and turning those pages.

The Pleasant Surprise

Here is the *pleasant* surprise. In an entire decision set, rarely will they ask more than two to three questions that will actually require you to go back and look at the data. The rest of the questions will be generic in nature, similar to questions in any other decision set. That is the surprise benefit of not getting yourself worked up over the data or playing The What If? Game. Just go see what they really *are* asking. This keeps your anxiety down, your productivity up, and the clock as your friend instead of your enemy.

When you do come to the questions that actually have you look at the data, you do not have to be a statistical whiz. They are looking for *entry-level* data analysis knowledge and skills. Therefore, if they ask you where a large or the larg*est* need in the district, grade, or content area is, look for the *lowest* scores or those on a downward trend. Low scores indicate need for improvement. As shown in Figure 13.1, downward trends indicate we are going the wrong direction and require immediate intervention to turn them around.

Even the best districts have a lowest area in *something*. Until every district has 100% mastery of every concept on every test, there is always a need to improve. This is a classic example of being a reflective and data-sensitive leader. Every superintendent, principal, teacher, and member of the district community must continuously be asking themselves and others, "How can we do *this* better?" The *this* is generic. It makes no difference if we are discussing math scores, band competitions, or the Pillsbury

Figure 13.1 Identifying District Strengths, Weaknesses, and Trends

Low Scores	⟶	Areas of Weakness
High Scores	⟶	Areas of Strength
Moving Scores	⟶	Potential Trends

Photo courtesy of Greg Wilmore, Helen and Wes Nelson

Bake-Off. Until every student masters every objective, we are not there yet. We are not through seeking improvement. We do not have time to rest on our laurels and think as Scarlet O'Hara did, "I'll think about it tomorrow at Tara." We must lead our districts *today* to prepare educated, informed, and productive citizens necessary for the American democratic society of tomorrow.

However, we cannot wait till tomorrow to think about the difficult tasks ahead of us. We cannot procrastinate. We must always and forever be asking, "How can we/I do this better?" Identify it, and do it. There are no excuses. Excuses are for losers. *You* will lead districts that are *winners.* There is no time to waste. To enhance student performance as measured by standardized test scores, you must know how to read, analyze, draw conclusions about, and facilitate the implementation and assessment of programs, curriculum, instructional strategies, and personnel that will meet the needs of today's students in your district. Do not focus unduly on what is working elsewhere. That is not your job. Your job is to create the best organizational culture and climate to facilitate maximized student performance in your district. The answers to where the areas are to address are in the data. No two schools or districts are exactly alike. Your role is to know your data inside out, to be able to speak fluently and coherently about it to anyone who will listen, and to always be thinking of new and better ways to engage and enhance student learning.

If a question steers you toward areas of *growth* within a district, grade, or content area, you will look at the numbers to see the greatest difference in a *positive,* not a negative direction. If a question asks you where a district's *greatest strengths* are, look for the *bigger numbers* or the areas showing the *greatest upward trends.* It could be that one category of concepts or a certain grade is still higher than another, *but* those scores are stagnant or even regressing a tiny bit. At the same time, another area may be showing consistent, steady, albeit slow, growth. If the numbers are consistently coming up, even if it is slowly, that is a positive thing and should be noticed, praised, and supplemented. Watch for answers that catch trends like that. The test developers love to throw in responses that determine if you are utilizing higher order thinking skills by catching trends or implications. Show them you are by selecting the correct response.

You will not be asked any detailed or advanced statistical analysis questions. That is not the primary role of the superintendent and certainly not a beginning superintendent. The test will not ask you about variances or standard deviations, so relax. They do want to know that you know how to determine if students in your district are learning and what their strengths and weaknesses are and that you are leading planning processes to increase student performance based on the scores presented. If students from *all* subgroups are not learning, why aren't they?

What can be done to improve the culture, climate, instruction, and curriculum of the district such that *all* students can and do learn? Therefore, the purpose of any testing is threefold. It is to

- measure student growth;
- assess student, campus, and district strengths, weaknesses, and trends; and
- utilize data as a sound basis for determining goals for student growth and improvement for the district, campus, grade, and content areas.

Last, remember, it does not matter how high the preponderance of your students' scores if *everyone* is not learning. Remember, this test is about *all* students, not just some of them. Ideal Superintendents never, ever, ever give up until *every* student is mastering every concept. District excellence is not determined by the scores of students who are motivated and easy to teach. District excellence is determined by the success of all students in all areas. Excellence is for everyone. Do you think this philosophy is unrealistic? Fine. Just remember, there are other jobs available for those who lose sight of the ideal. Places outside education are hiring. They have plenty of jobs for those who only want a paycheck and do not have a passion for excellence in learning for everyone to further the promulgation of an enhanced American democratic society. As for you, you are on your own quest for educational excellence. If you are not on this quest, on the day of the test, *pretend* you are! This test is about excellence for all. If you do not truly believe this can be attained, you will not pass this test. If you do believe all students can and will learn provided the right curriculum, instruction, resources, and support services, you are on your way to being a cutting-edge, highly effective superintendent.

HOW TO READ AND INTERPRET AN "ACADEMIC EXCELLENCE INDICATOR SYSTEM" REPORT

Whereas students all across America in both public and private districts take achievement tests, the Academic Excellence Indicator System (AEIS) is exclusive to Texas. Every campus and district is rated in this important accountability system based largely on data detailed in the annual AEIS report. Two important areas are student passing rates on the TAKS and student attendance. However, do not be surprised if you see references to the precursor of TAKS, which was called the Texas Assessment of Academic Skills (TASS). Some questions or decision sets may have not yet been updated. This will have no impact on how you answer questions since both tests were built around increasing student performance for all students. Results from both are presented in the same way on AEIS reports.

As you begin looking at any AEIS report, let us first look at the overall report to see what you have been presented. There are *three specific areas* to consider. You may or may not be given each of these areas to analyze, but you want to know about all of them, just in case. First is the cover or title page. It will tell you the academic year of testing, as well as the name, district number, and state rating of the overall district.

The subsequent report is divided into two sections. There are certain things that always appear in each section and never are changed. Memorize them. Please notice this is the first time I have asked you to memorize anything. I did not ask you to memorize any of the ten competencies. I asked you to fully understand and comprehend them so you would recognize what the test developers are questioning you about. Yet now I am asking you to memorize the short lists presented in Figure 13.2. By memorizing what is found where, as shown in Figure 13.2, you will

Figure 13.2 Components of an AEIS Report

SECTION I:

Test Data
Attendance

SECTION II:

Student Information (except testing)
Staff Information
Budget Information
Program Information

Photo courtesy of Dr. Tom Parks, Dr. James Laub, Joyce Laub, Greg and Dr. Elaine Wilmore, Dr. David Thompson, Dr. Bruce Barnett

save time and anxiety in searching through a report to find the data you need to make informed responses to your test questions.

The simplest way to remember what is located where is to know that everything about testing and attendance is in Section I. *Everything else is in Section II.* Therefore, when determining where to look for an appropriate answer, if the question has something to do with test scores or student attendance, you know the answer will be in Section I. You can thus ignore Section II for this question.

However, if the question does not relate to testing or student attendance, go straight to Section II and look in the appropriate category there. Section I always and forever will only have information regarding student TAAS or TAKS performance and attendance, so your answer will not be there. For ease in navigating the report, the section and page numbers are listed in the top right corner of each page. Now let's look deeper into what these things mean.

Section I of an AEIS Report: Student Testing Data

The first section of the AEIS report addresses everything you would ever want to know, or not want to know, about student performance on TAAS or TAKS. It is presented in a chart format. TAAS or TAKS begins in the third grade and continues through various versions throughout high school. It was originally given primarily in reading, math, and writing with secondary districts also reporting "End of Course Test" results. Subsequently, tests in both science and social studies were added. Some subjects, such as writing, science, and social studies, are not given in every grade; thus, there will not be any scores reported for the grades in which they are not given.

The student groups are listed at the top of the chart from left to right with the largest subgroup coming first and going in decreasing size to the various demographic subgroups. For the sake of our discussion, let's say that we are presented with an AEIS report that is looking at third-grade reading and math scores, since writing is not given in the third grade. It is helpful to think "big to little" in looking at each subgroup and how it performed. Individual student scores are never known on either a campus or district AEIS report. That data is provided on the campus level and protected by privacy laws. In other words, while you may go online to see how any district and campus in Texas did on their AEIS report, you cannot determine how Little Johnny Next Door did on his tests. It will not be there. If you are asked any question that seeks to check your knowledge of student privacy and confidentiality, the answer is the public does *not* get to see or access individual student records.

The biggest group is the *State*, so state results will appear in the first column. Under this column, the scores of students per grade and subject will be provided. In our example of third grade, the column will show how all third graders in Texas did on reading and math. Everyone, and especially the press, wants to compare and contrast how your district did in comparison to the overall state. No one wants to be below the state average in any area.

The next column will be the *District Group*. The *District Group* is also exceedingly important. It is second in importance only to the column that is your *District*. What is the *District Group*? Each year, detailed demographic data about every student in every district as well as data about the district itself are entered by staff (not you, thank goodness) into the Big State Computer in the Clouds called PEIMS. The Big State Computer in the Clouds crunches all the numbers and codes for various factors such as race, gender, student age, grade, socioeconomics, mobility, district wealth, and so forth. Each campus and district is subsequently given an opportunity to correct erroneous information at specific points during the year to assure data accuracy. As a superintendent and principal, it is in your best interest for this information to be perfect because this is what is used to determine your *District Group*. The *District Group* includes the districts in the state that are the *most similar* to yours according to all the factors indicated above for PEIMS. You want to be in the correct district group because your district's performance will be compared and contrasted to these fine folks in your good old AEIS report.

You may wonder why that is such a big deal. Let me explain it to you. Let's say that you are superintendent of Poor Me Independent School District (ISD). Poor Me ISD is, gee, rather pitiful. For example, 100% of the students are eligible for free or reduced-priced lunch. No one speaks English. No one lives in a single-family dwelling. In fact, virtually everyone lives in low-rent property and moves all the time. Thus, students at your district are constantly changing and rarely get to establish many roots. Few of the homes have two parents in them. Unemployment, alcohol, and drugs abound. For the sake of discussion, I am overexaggerating, but you get the point. Poor Me ISD has had dismal scores on all forms of student testing for years and has earned sympathy from everyone because, gee, they are a rather pitiful lot. Who could expect them to perform very well academically? They have been pitiful and gotten by with it without too much protest. Poor Me ISD is your classic example of low expectations and reaping what you sow. If you do not think a student, campus, or district will produce much, guess what: They won't. Fortunately, the opposite is also true. If we know that to be true, why do we not expect high performance out of everyone?

Well! The *District Group* addresses that. Poor Me ISD is now being compared to *other* districts whose demographics look just like its demographics. What superintendent would want to have to explain to the school board, or the community, why its students perform worse than other districts that look *just like them* and have almost identical circumstances? The net result is, when the *District Group*, as well as the *Campus Group* on campus AEIS reports went into effect, scores went up in all districts including the Poor Me ISDs. Welcome to the age of high-stakes accountability in a No Child Left Behind world.

Now that you have done such a good job improving student performance as superintendent of Poor Me ISD, you have been solicited to apply, and ultimately get, the superintendent position at Pretty Good ISD. Pretty Good ISD is in the same geographic area as Poor Me ISD, but that is all they have in common. At Pretty Good ISD, there is no rental property. Everyone owns their home and is proud of it. Everyone speaks English and maybe another couple of languages just for fun. No one qualifies for free or reduced-priced lunch. There is virtually no mobility. In fact, parents of kindergarteners are already requesting the teachers they want their children to have in first, second, or third grade! Almost every home has two parents plus maybe a maid or a nanny. No one rides the bus because children walk or ride their bikes safely to school, or neighborhood car pools pick them up to take them to Scouts, soccer practice, gymnastics, or piano lessons. Along the way, they will stop and have a snow cone or ice cream. Life is so nice at Pretty Good ISD. Not surprisingly, so are the test scores. They are pretty good.

But they are not excellent. Administrators, faculty, staff, and even the school board members at Pretty Good ISD have been content with their district's pretty good scores. After all, they *always* outperform those poor, pitiful little children over at Poor Me ISD, God bless them. Here at Pretty Good ISD, students can do relatively well without too much extra effort. They look pretty good under the *State* and *District* columns, so what is the problem?

That is where the *District Group* comes in handy. Now scores from Pretty Good ISD are being compared to scores from other pretty good districts. Oops! What superintendent would like to have to explain to the school board and community why, although their scores are pretty good, they are *below* their *District Group* of other districts that look virtually just like them? This would not be a happy conversation. Therefore, instruction at all the pretty good district campuses also becomes much more focused and data driven. The result is improved curriculum, instruction, and assessment in the Pretty Good, Poor Me, and all other districts in the state. Although some consider the *District*

Group a headache, it actually is a good thing. It keeps all districts on their toes and cognizant of how other districts with similar demographics are doing. The net results are improved learning and accountability for everyone. In simple language, the *District Group* holds all of us accountable for teaching and learning every day. If a superintendent is not leading and facilitating improved student learning for truly altruistic reasons, the AEIS report should take care of it.

The *District* column is, obviously, your own district's scores. Although it is not the first column in the "big to little" sequence, it is the first column you look at because, honey, it is yours. State law now requires student performance scores from the district AEIS report to be used in the superintendent's annual evaluation. Believe me, the scores presented here are of the utmost importance to your job security. Highlight your district's scores in yellow. Study and think about them almost 24 hours of the day. These data should be critical elements in guiding all subsequent analysis and discussion of district needs and goal setting. How will you lead your district personnel, as well as the community, to improve student performance based on these and campus-level data? What are other important sources of data that should be included in district strategic planning?

After the *District* column, still thinking "big to little," the columns are divided into various student subgroups. These include *African American, Hispanic, White, Native American, Asian/Pacific Islanders, Male, Female, Economically Disadvantaged,* and *Special Education.* The goal is for *every* subgroup to do well, including Special Education. You do not want to see any large differences in passing rates of students on any section of any test. If you do, you and your district-community *must* ask yourself *why,* and then create plans and strategies to resolve the discrepancies. In the Ideal District, instruction is individualized and curriculum is developmentally appropriate such that there will be no significant deviations between subgroups. When, in reality, there are deviations, intense study and planning are undertaken by many stakeholders to resolve the situation such that *all* students learn with maximized performance for their varying ability levels. This is not simply an idealistic philosophy. It is reality in today's schools and districts.

Those are all of the categories placed into columns. Along the left side of each page in Section I will be rows labeled with the subjects tested such as reading, math, writing, science, social studies, or *All Tests.* Appropriate scores will be noted on two lines for the current year and the previous year. In each area, you will want your scores to be coming *up* annually, not going down. If they are going down or remaining stagnant, again, you and your district-community must analyze *why* and plan for both short- and long-term improvement.

The *All Tests* is an interesting row. It is there to determine the percentage of students who passed every test they took. It is necessary because if you just looked at the individual subjects and compared results, you would get a less than complete picture. For example, let's go back to our hypothetical set of district third-grade scores. Say 50% of the third graders passed reading, and 50% of the grade passed math. At first glance, you might think, "Well, 50% of the students in third grade are doing really well. The other 50% cannot read or do math."

This could be a wrong conclusion. What if it was a *different* set of students that passed each portion?

- What if 50% of them actually have the ability to read *War and Peace* but could not successfully add 2 + 2?
- What if the other 50% could work algorithms but could not read *The Cat in the Hat?*

Hmm. We have a problem here. This problem is why we have the *All Tests* row. It allows us to see an overall picture of exactly what percentage of the district is passing *everything* taken. The goal is to have 100% of the students passing all tests.

The first portion of Section I will always be set up in this format. Therefore, this is where you would look if you were asked any questions that relate to specific grade-level or subgroup performance on any test for any grade or for the district as a whole. If you are asked to compare scores, ascertain trends, or identify strengths or weaknesses of performance, this is also where you would look.

The next portion of Section I is a summary of all the scores in the district. The rows and columns of the chart remain the same. It will say *TAAS/TAKS % Passing Sum of 3–8 & 10.* If the district you are analyzing is quite small and does not have all those grades, it does not matter. This chart is simply a quick reference guide to the overall performance of how the entire district did on the specified subjects and *All Tests.* If you are asked any questions about overall district performance, this is where you would look first.

At the bottom of this portion will be an important section labeled *TAAS/TAKS% Exempted Sum of 3–8 & 10.* This is important because although it will be wonderful if you have 100% passing rates in every category above, if you have exempted half the district, it is not a good sign! School boards, as well as the state itself, look at this closely. They do not want you exempting high percentages of students. Their goal is for everyone to test and score well. Therefore, this section will show the percentage of students, per subgroup, that you have exempted for any reason, including special education or limited English proficiency (LEP) purposes. Again, it is *very important* for you to have low percentages in this area. Special education students must now test via TAKS or an alternative method, and scores are reported. This is one of the few places that you want your numbers to be *less* than the *State, District,* or *Campus Group.* You particularly do *not* want high percentages of exemptions or bad scores within any of your subgroups. Again, the goal is for everyone to test and everyone to do well.

Section I of an AEIS Report: Student Attendance

The last portion of Section I is *Attendance.* Attendance is important because if students are not coming to school, it is difficult for them to maximize their learning opportunities . . . or at least the things you want them to learn. The same format for grouping columns previously described is also used here. The important thing to notice is that the two years listed are always one year behind. That is not an accident, nor is it placed there to confuse you. The reason is simple. This academic year is not over yet; therefore, it is impossible to determine the total percentage of attendance. Obviously, you want your attendance percentages to be *higher* than your *State* or *District Group.* You do want to see high attendance percentage rates among all district subgroups. If a certain subgroup has low attendance, it is critically important to ascertain *why.* Why are these students not coming to school? What can we as a district or community do to address this situation? Again, if students are not in attendance, it is going to be very difficult for them to learn. Also, since this is Texas and we have a rule or regulation for everything, if attendance becomes too low or dropout rates become too high, the district will be cited by the State with very serious consequences. These consequences, if not addressed, could result in the district receiving bad ratings, being put under a state "master" for leadership, or ultimately being closed. Needless to say, these are not things any district wants to have happen. A major goal of a democratic society is to produce literate, cognizant, contributing citizens. This is hard to do when students are not in school.

Section II of an AEIS Report

A simple way to remember what is in Section II is that it has everything that is *not* in Section I. While that may appear obvious, it is very easy to remember the two things that are in Section I. They are student testing and student attendance. Therefore, if you are asked a question that does *not* relate to testing or attendance, go straight to Section II. A quick reminder hint is that if you ever get lost in the pages of an AEIS report, the quickest way to find out where you are is to look at the top right corner of each page. It will say if you are in Section I or Section II. Let's now see what *is* in Section II. We already know it is *not* testing or attendance information!

The first segment of Section II is *Student Information.* Everything is still presented in chart format. The subgroups no longer appear. The basic layout will be *District, District Group,* and *State.* You will be given basic student enrollment (*not testing*) information such as how many students and what percentage of your enrollment is in each grade and campus of the district. It will be further disaggregated into *Ethnic Distribution, Mobility, Economically Disadvantaged, Limited English Proficient, Number of Students per Teacher,* and *Retention Rates.* This will be charted in rows comparing this district to their *District Group* and the *State.* Other than *Number of Students per Teacher* and *Retention Rates by Grade* for both regular and special education students, there is no doing better or worse than these groups here. These are merely facts. However, you would like to see a small ratio of students to teachers as well as a *small* percentage of student retention. Although this section does not relate to testing, it is an important place to look when you are analyzing a report. Just as you do not want high passing rates due to high exemption rates, you also do not want high passing rates due to flunking everybody (found in this portion of Section II). This is the kind of critical thinking that test developers like to see if you will catch. Watch for it. We want everyone doing well on TAKS, of course, but *not* because the district exempted or flunked everyone at risk of not passing the test. Basically though, if you are given a question that pertains to *Enrollment, Ethnic Distribution, Mobility, Economically Disadvantaged, Limited English Proficiency, Number of Students per Teacher,* or *Retention Rates by Grade* for either regular or special education students, then the *Student Information* chart of Section II is where you would look. Remember this is where to find it for test-taking day.

The next section of Section II is *Staff Information.* It is set up in the same *Count, Percent, District Group* and *State* format as *Student Information.* This is where you will look to determine numbers and percentages of staff that are *Professional* (teachers, professional support, and campus administration), plus *Educational Aides, Total Staff, Total Minority Staff, Teachers by Ethnicity and Sex, Teachers by Years of Experience, Average Years of Experience of Teachers, Average Years of Experience of Teachers with District, Average*

Teacher Salary by Years of Experience and *Average Actual Salaries* for teachers, professional support, and campus administration. These data are public information and freely available to any citizen who wants to see them either by hard copy or via the Internet. The AEIS report brings various data together in one report.

If you are asked any questions regarding average salaries for virtually anyone, this is where you would look. If you were asked questions that involve planning for future personnel needs, one place to check would be to look at the average years of experience of district staff to begin thinking about future retirements and their potential effect on staffing, the budget, and instruction. This is where you would look to see how well your district is doing in comparison to the others in recruiting and retaining minority staff. This is a pressing issue for all districts. Because this is such a common issue statewide, watch for it as a common theme that could appear on the test.

For virtually any question you may have that relates to staffing, the *Staff Information* segment within Section II is where you would look first. Always think, "Is there any place else I could look for something that could be of importance to answering this, or any, question?" Remember, the competencies refer to using multiple sources of data repeatedly. By becoming familiar with exactly where to find what you're looking for in the AEIS report, you can utilize multiple pieces of information from within the same document to make an intelligent, data-driven decision.

The next component in Section II is *Budgeted Operating Expenditure Information*. This is where you will find everything about the budget in a summarized form. The format will again compare the *District, District Group* and *State*. A rule of thumb is that superintendents, school boards, and especially taxpayers like test scores to be *higher* than anyone else's, but for the district to be doing it with *less* money. Using that rationale, this, plus student retention and the teacher/student ratio, are the places you would like your numbers to be *less* than your comparison groups. The first place was in Section I in *TAAS/TAKS % Exempted Sum of 3–8 & 10*. We discussed it again in *Number of Students per Teacher* and *Retention Rates by Grade*. When it comes to money, always look for financial *prudence*. This is particularly true in relation to administrative costs. Boards and taxpayers like to see money targeted directly toward students and instruction and as little as possible toward administration. Within the *Budgeted Operating Expenditure Information* you will find the actual amount and percentage of the budget for the *Total District Budget* by *Function* and *Per Pupil*. Think, "Scores up, costs down." Remember this when looking at both budgets and test results. Remember this especially on the day you take your TExES exam.

The last chart in Section II is *Program Information*. This is where you will find how many students are in each category of the district program as well as the amount of money spent on each. *Program Information* uses the consistent Section II chart format of columns for *Count, Percent, District Group, District,* and *State.* The rows then provide the categories. These are *Student Enrollment by Program* for *Special Education, Career & Technology Education, Bilingual/ESL Education,* and *Gifted & Talented Education.* It provides the numbers and percentages of *Teachers by Program* for *Regular, Special, Compensatory, Career & Technology, Bilingual/ESL, Gifted & Talented,* and *Other.* Next, it details the *Budgeted Instructional Operating Expenditures by Program* for each. If you are asked questions about program equity, particularly in the area of finance, this would be where you would first look.

My last suggestion for you in data analysis is to utilize your common sense. Think prudently when improving student performance is your basic guiding principle in every instance. That is what they are looking for, so show it to them in your answer choices.

SUMMARY

In closing our study of data analysis through standardized tests and AEIS reports, remember to do these things:

- Look to see the profile of what you have been given. What kind of test or what portion of an AEIS report has been provided for your review?
- What concepts or components are made available?
- Do *not* play The What If? Game. Do *not* try to be psychic by trying to draw conclusions about the data *before* you read each question. Turn the page, and *read* the questions. Then you will know where to look and what to analyze per question.
- The test is looking only for *entry-level* data analysis skills. Keep your anxiety level down so your productivity will stay *up.*
- Practice looking at various standardized test results and AEIS reports within your own district or on the Internet before the TExES exam so that you will be familiar and comfortable with forms and layout.
- Memorize what goes in Sections I and II of an AEIS report. This will save you time and anxiety on the day you test because you will know exactly where to look for the answers.

Assuming you have one or more decision sets relating to an AEIS report, look to see if you have a Section I, Section II, or both. Similar to standardized test results, you will look at the overview of what you have been given. The top right corner of every page will provide this information. You can easily remember what types of information will be found in *Section I.* It is basically *testing and attendance. Everything else* is in *Section II.* Go directly to the questions to see exactly what they are asking rather than playing The What If? Game of what they *might* ask. This saves time, effort, and anxiety.

Knowing and becoming familiar with the *format* of an AEIS report plus knowing what will always be in Sections I and II turn a scary and sometimes formidable portion of the TExES exam into a very workable passage. Remember, Section I has testing and attendance. Everything else is in Section II. Knowing this and making yourself familiar with multiple AEIS reports from various districts before the test will help you walk into your test *cool, calm, collected, confident, and almost downright cocky.* This confidence level is what you want as you *ace* this test.

14

Test-Taking Strategies

It is assumed that students who are preparing for the superintendent TExES examination have had an appropriate university or alternative preparation program in district leadership. The goal of this book is to enhance that foundation and to help you pass the TExES examination. The purpose is not to reteach your certification program. Therefore, assuming you have the prerequisite knowledge base necessary *and* you utilize the philosophy and skills presented in this book, you should *ace* this test. That means you should be able to walk in to take the TExES exam cool, calm, collected, confident, and almost downright cocky. Anxiety is not your friend. As shown in Figure 14.1, when your anxiety goes up, your productivity goes down. The reverse is also true.

The test, from this point on, is a mind game. You have the knowledge and conceptual framework to knock the top out of this test. Therefore, what you think you will achieve, you will achieve. If you think you will pass the test, you will. If you think you will not, you won't. Either way, you will be right. Your mind is the front wheel of the wheelbarrow that leads your life. Go forward with a positive mind-set. Here are strategies to help you.

THE LAYOUT OF THE DAY

Morning Session: The District Profile Packet

The superintendent TExES exam is structured differently from any of the other TExES exams. First, it lasts all day rather than a portion of

Figure 14.1   Anxiety and Productivity Do Not Work Well Together

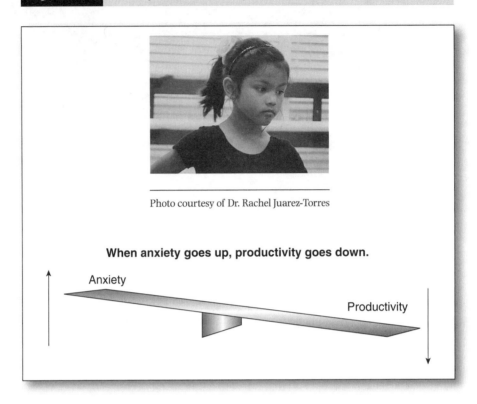

Photo courtesy of Dr. Rachel Juarez-Torres

When anxiety goes up, productivity goes down.

Anxiety

Productivity

the day. It is divided into a specific morning session and a totally different afternoon session. You may not go back and forth answering questions from the sections at any time. The morning session will have questions that address a series of data you will be given called the District Profile Packet. This packet from an imaginary school district will contain various forms of data a superintendent can expect to see during the course of any given period. These could include calendars, board agenda packets or other board issues, phone calls, test data, financial problems, legal responses, unhappy parents, irate citizens . . . you name it, there could be something about it in your packet. Everything in the packet will in some way address one or more of the ten competencies we have been studying. Organize the items from your packet as if you were really a superintendent. What would be the most pressing issues? Which would you have to address first? Which items would require you obtaining more information before you could make a data-driven response? From whom would you need to get that information? Use whatever organizational schema works best for you, but do organize the data. Spend the first significant time of the morning session reading, organizing, and getting a good grasp of exactly what data you have before you start to read the questions. Organizational guru Stephen Covey (1990) reminds us to sharpen the saw before we begin virtually anything. In this instance, the time you spend studying, analyzing, sorting, and organizing your data is sharpening your saw. It will be time very well spent before you begin answering the test questions. If you do not spend this time effectively and efficiently, you will lose productivity during the remainder of the morning session, as you have to go back, read, and sort to find what is needed to answer the questions appropriately. If you do these things first, once you begin addressing the questions, you will have the data and the big picture of the district already in your mind and at your fingertips. Reading, sorting, and organizing first is not a waste of time. It is your key to success in the morning session. Sharpen your saw well. After that, respond to these questions as you would any others:

- As an Ideal Superintendent
- Making data-driven and student-focused decisions
- Aligned with the theoretical framework (three domains and ten competencies)
- Utilizing the 1–2–3–4 Plan
- Watching for the key concepts, the "Sherry list" as shown in Chapter 2, Figure 2.2

Afternoon Session: Analytical and Problem-Solving Skills

Your afternoon session will consist of multiple-decision sets similar to what you experienced on the Principal TExES exam. Each decision set is composed of a prompt, followed by related questions. When you begin this section, you will read the prompt that introduces the first decision set. Remember, there are no questions or answers in the prompt. The prompt simply tells you a little bit about the district or situation you will be addressing. As you read, underline words that you think are important. You are allowed to write in your test booklet. You do not get bonus points for turning in a clean booklet, so utilize your visual and kinesthetic senses by underlining key words or important concepts throughout TExES. This will help you stay focused on what the question is really asking and not allow you to become distracted by potentially great responses that do not happen to answer *this* question.

There are specific strategies that will help you. Thus far, you have studied a lot for the superintendent TExES exam. Now it is time to learn other test-taking techniques to help you win this mind game and, subsequently, knock the top off this test.

THE DOT GAME: A PSYCHOLOGICAL AND TIME MANAGEMENT STRATEGY

You will have plenty of time to successfully complete this exam. There is no reason for you to run out of time. However, on rare occasion, I hear of someone who claims they did. I am going to teach you to utilize a deceptively simple technique called The Dot Game. If you play The Dot Game, it will be impossible for you to run out of time. Here is how to do it.

After reading the prompt for your first decision set, you will read the first question. You will mark the answer. You will read the next question. You will mark the answer. This will go along just fine until you get to a question where you really are not sure of the answer. This question is one of those that make you go, "Hmmmmm." This happens to everyone so do not feel bad. Read the question and possible answers again. If you still do not feel confident about which is the correct response, put a dot by the question and move on. Just skip that question. Do not feel guilty. Do not look back. Just put the dot by it and keep on moving. Don't worry. The Dot Game has steps. You will be coming back to this question, and any others you leave a dot by, later.

Continue until you hit another question where you are not sure of the answer. Put a dot by it, too. Do not spend over two minutes pondering the right answer to any question. The longer you spend trying to figure out the answer, the more your anxiety level will go up. When your anxiety level goes up, your productivity goes down. Worse, the clock is ticking. The clock is not your friend. I am your friend, so listen to me! Put a dot by it, and go on to the next question.

Repeat this process throughout the entire afternoon session. I do not care if you have thirty dots when you finish. Big deal. You have accomplished something significant: You have worked your way through the entire test. You know every question and concept they have to throw at you. You've seen it all. The pressure is off.

Here is what I want you to do when you finish going through the test this first time. Close your book. Get up. Go to the restroom. Shake out the tenseness in your muscles. Get a drink of water. Walk around for a minute or two to clear your head and relax. It will be time well spent to rid your body and mind of tension and stress and to loosen up. Then, before you go back in, stop and say out loud to utilize your auditory sense, "Thank goodness I have made it through this test *the first time.* Now I am going back in there to *finish acing this baby!"* Do not ignore what I am saying. It is important that your subconscious *hear* you affirm that you are going to pass this test. Repeat it over and over, out loud and silently. It is all a part of winning the mind game.

When you go back into the testing room, only return to the questions where you have dots. Remember, when anxiety goes down, productivity goes up (Figure 14.1). Because of that, you will be pleasantly surprised to see how many of them you will be able to answer quickly this time simply due to four reasons:

- The pressure is off. You have all ready seen everything on the test. There is nothing scary left. Psychologically, your subconscious has begun to relax; thus, your productivity will go up.
- You know that, in this instance, you do not have to make 100 on the TExES exam to pass it. Districts do not really care what your score is. They only care if you are certified. A passing score on TExES, plus other certification requirements, will accomplish that goal.
- There is something odd that happens after you have read the entire test. The *philosophy* as well as *key words and phrases* will settle into your subconscious and become familiar. If you have *not* spent too long pondering the difficult questions, generally the second time through, the appropriate answers will reveal themselves to you quickly. This is not as likely to happen if you have spent too long pondering each question when you read the question initially.
- You are no longer fighting the clock. You know you have already answered the ones that you are certain of. You do not have to stress over getting through the whole test the first time without running out of time. With this additional pressure off, your mind is freed to better comprehend what the more difficult questions are asking you.

If you do not have all the answers after your second time through, it is perfectly all right. Repeat the process. Close your book. Take a break, just like you did before. Your anxiety level should be *way* down by now because you know that you do not need to make 100. Just passing will do.

Regardless, keep repeating The Dot Game until you have answered all the questions. If that is over three times, guess on the ones you are not sure of and go home. This test is not the GRE. You are not penalized for wrong answers. It is unlikely you will have a divine intervention to tell you the right answers at this point. There is no sense in sitting there forever pondering a question that you are clueless about. Move on.

If you will play The Dot Game, there is no way that you can run out of time. If you do *not* play The Dot Game, you will lose time and productivity on some questions, resulting in leaving a stack of easy questions unanswered. While you sit there stewing over Number 16, the clock is ticking away. Worse, your chances of getting Number 16 correct are going down because your anxiety level is going up. Do not do that. Just play The Dot Game as directed, and keep your forward progress moving.

There are some students who are simply slow readers or have difficulty with reading comprehension. This is often particularly true for test takers whose first language is not English. In these cases, The Dot Game is particularly beneficial. This test is long, has a lot of reading, and necessitates excellent comprehension skills. If you do not totally understand what is being asked, how can you expect to pick the right answer? Therefore, I strongly suggest that if you are a slow reader or if you have issues with reading comprehension that you check into getting some help right away. Don't wait till the week of the test when there is little that can be done. Try talking to a reading teacher for suggestions and then follow them. Another good idea is to take a reading comprehension or speed-reading course through community education, a local community college, or online. Regardless, it is *imperative* that you play The Dot Game to keep you moving and focused. You do not want to run out of time while you are still trying to figure out the second decision set.

Last, in the unlikely event that you have played The Dot Game two or three times and for whatever reason you suddenly fall into a coma until a test monitor comes to shake you awake and tell you it is time to leave, here is what you do: Guess. Guess like crazy, and do it quick before they throw you out. Then go seek medical attention about your coma.

This is very important: There are no correct answers left blank. You must put *something* down to have a *chance* of getting it right. Any chance beats no chance, so guess like crazy. You are not penalized for wrong answers. You do get credit for correct answers. If you get it right due to blind luck, congratulations. Pick the most ideal response to create the most ideal situation. Remember to forget reality and to think ideal. The developers of this test want to know if you know how to lead a district in an ideal manner. That is the goal behind every question. Therefore, forget how you have seen someone else respond to a similar situation in real life unless that person was performing in an ideal manner. The number one mistake people make on this test is to pick answers based on reality, things they have seen done in real life. Forget that. In response to every question ask yourself, "What is the most ideal response?" Once you have identified the most ideal response, you have the answer to the question even if it does sound Pollyanna-ish.

That, my friends, is how to play The Dot Game. It is deceptively simple. Play it and win. It will help you stay cool, calm, collected, confident, and almost downright cocky. More importantly, it will help you manage the clock and your stress and will help you ace this test the first time you take it!

THE DOG AND STAR GAME: A DECISION-MAKING STRATEGY

The afternoon session of the superintendent TExES exam is multiple choice. You do not need to memorize facts. You *do* need to be able to synthesize and apply the philosophy of the ten competencies we discussed in Chapters 3 through 12 as well as the strategies presented here. There will be four answer choices. In the best of times, one of them will shout at you as being correct. That answer is a star. We like stars. They make our lives easy. Still, since you will be such a good test taker, you want to make sure you are right. Therefore, when you find a really good answer, otherwise known as a star, draw a little star by that response in your booklet. But keep reading. Do you see any more really good answers? If so, mark them too. By process of elimination, one of those stars has to be brighter than the other. That means, in truth, one is a star while another is a baby star, a twinkle. Think to yourself, if I can only pick one of these meteorites, which one will it be? Which one is the brightest? Which one has more language from the competencies in it? Which response includes the most Important Points to Remember as provided as the end of Chapters 3 through 12? That response is the star. Mark it.

While we love stars, there is another group of responses that we like just about as much. They are dogs. Dogs are *bad* answers. Why would we be watching for bad answers? Because there are only four response choices. If one of them is a dog, utilize those good old kinesthetic and visual senses again and *draw a great big line through it.* As you progress through the test, you will take great pride in drawing *big, heavy lines* through those dogs. This is important for three reasons:

- Every time you identify a dog, your chances of getting the answer right go up by 25%.
- If you can find a dog *and* a puppy, mark both of them out. A puppy is another bad answer. It's just not quite as bad as the dog. But it is still wrong and you know it is wrong. By marking out both a dog and a puppy, you will increase your chances of getting the question right by 50%!

- It is good psychology for you to *feel and see* the results of this decision-making process. It adds to your subconscious confidence that you are attacking the test in a systematic and methodical manner, and that you are going to *pass* this test out of sheer diligence and conscientiousness. Therefore, be sure to draw a line through every answer you know is wrong. It's good psychology and helps you select the right answer.

Let's say that out of four potential choices, you did not find a star. However, as you are reading the responses, you find a twinkle, or a pretty good answer. You are not in love with it, but it will do. You also found a dog and a puppy. The other choice is just . . . there. There is not much for or against it. Or, as often happens, it is a perfectly good response. It just does not answer *this* question. They do that a lot. It tends to confuse people who think, "That is a good thing to do." Well, it may be. Just because a response says George Washington was the first president of the United States and you know that is true, does not mean it is the correct answer for this question. Beware! They love to throw in distracters like that, which are totally true. Do not let them trick you! If a response does not answer this question, it is a *wrong* response even if it is a good thing to do. Always bear in mind what *this question* is asking. That is why it is important to *underline key words or phrases in every question.* It helps to keep you focused on the *intent* of this question.

If you do not find a bright shining star, but you do find a twinkle, a puppy, a dog, and a non-issue, or distracter, your correct answer is the twinkle. It may not be an obvious meteorite like we love, but it will do. Mark it. It is the best choice available and will get the job done. We love stars, and we love dogs. We will settle for twinkles and puppies. Each time you can identify any of these, your chances of getting the question correct go up by 25%. If you can eliminate two, your chances go up by 50%. There will be many times when you can eliminate all three wrong choices. By process of elimination you now have the correct answer. Mega kudos!

MULTIPLE–MULTIPLES: TO MAXIMIZE SUCCESS, ALWAYS USE "THE PROCESS"

As we know, the entire test is multiple choice with four selections per problem. However, there are some questions that are more complex. They begin by presenting the question in the standard method. Next they list four potential solutions prefixed by roman numerals I, II, III, and IV. Beside those are the standard choices A, B, C, and D. The choices for A through D are various combinations of roman numerals I through IV.

These multiple-multiples drive some people crazy. I must admit that at one time I was against them. I felt they got away from the *intent* of the test, which is to determine entry level skills for a new superintendent, and that they put undue focus on reading comprehension and test-taking skills. However, it is not up to me to write the test. This is the test as we have it today. We cannot change it, but we sure can pass it. We have the now-famous Elaine Wilmore Process. Memorize and practice The Process. It is about to become your new best friend.

Here is an example of how to use The Process. Stick with me here. We are going to do several examples to make sure you understand The Process.

Example: What is/are Dr. Wilmore's
favorite thing(s) to eat?

I. Raw minnows disguised as sushi

II. Broccoli

III. Italian food

IV. Chocolate (YUMMY!)

    A. I, II
    B. II
    C. I, II, III
    D. IV

The above sample question requires you to know a little about my eating preferences. Here are some hints.

1. I do not eat raw fish of any kind. (Dog answer.)

2. I do like broccoli, but it is far from being my *favorite* food. (This would be a puppy response due to the key word being "favorite." In choosing answers be sure to look closely at every word. Your clue this time was "favorite.")

3. I have been to Italy four times and really, really like Italian food. (Twinkle response. Reading up to this point, it would be the best choice . . . but you keep reading to see *all* your options.)

4. Life is short. I can't live it without chocolate. In times of high stress . . . chocolate. In times of celebration . . . chocolate. Needing a pick-me-up for the sheer pleasure of it . . . chocolate. There are no bad kinds of chocolate. All chocolate is good. The world resolves around chocolate. (Chocolate is a *star* answer!!!!! It takes nothing away from the Italian food. Italian food is still wonderful. By not

selecting Italian food, we are not saying it isn't a good answer. It is just not the *best* answer. On the TExES exam, you are looking for the *best* answer or the brightest star. In this instance, chocolate is outshining Italian food, dadgummit.)

STEPS IN THE PROCESS

1. Do nothing till you are *sure*.

The first thing you will do on a "multiple-multiple" question is nothing till you are sure. So, after reading this question, you would look at the first, or I, response. It says, "Raw minnows disguised as sushi." Since you know I do not eat raw fish of any kind, you are *positive* (e.g., "sure") this could not possibly be my favorite food. Draw a line through Option I because we know it is not right. Since we are *sure,* you go to the *next step* in The Process. *That step* is not *reading the next response! Never skip steps! The key to The Process working so well is to follow it! Do not ever skip steps!*

2. Go straight to the *bottom*.

Since we are sure the first response is not the right answer, we now go straight to the A, B, C, D answers at the *bottom.*

- Look at Option A. Do we see a I in it? Yes, we do. Since there is a I in it and we are sure I is not the right answer, draw a line through all of Option A. It is a wrong response regardless of the rest of it. You have now improved your chances of getting this question correct by 25%. But we are not through.
- Look at Option B. Does it have a 1 in it? No, it does not. Since it does not have a 1 in it, we keep it. Don't draw a line through it.
- Look at Option C. Does it have a 1 in it? Yes, it does. Guess what we do. We draw a line through it because it cannot be the right answer. Now we have eliminated two of the possible answer choices while only having read item I. We have improved your chances of getting this question right by 50%.
- Look at Option D. Does it have a I in it? No, it does not, so we keep it. We know the answer will be either Option B or Option D.
- Move forward to the next step in The Process . . .

3. *Compare and contrast* the remaining options.

In our case, the remaining options are B and D. We do *not* immediately return to the top food choices. We compare and contrast the choices in B and D. Option B is broccoli. We think broccoli could be a decent answer, but we doubt it is my *favorite* food. Since we are not *sure* (see Step 1 of The Process.), we take a look at Option D.

Option D is chocolate!!! We know I love me some chocolate! We also know it would be exceedingly unlikely for me to like broccoli more than chocolate. Since we have now compared and contrasted B and D and are *sure* about D, the correct answer is D.

At this point you may be asking yourself, what about Option C? In this case, it was totally irrelevant. It did not end up mattering that I do like Italian food a lot. It could just as well have said the sun comes up in the east. It's a "That's nice" response that simply does not matter because we followed The Process and did not skip steps!

Now, what would have happened if you had not followed The Process? If you had read all the options first instead of doing nothing till you are *sure*, the whole Italian thing would have confused you because you know I do like it. But by following The Process *exactly*, you knew the Italian food had no relevance at all.

Let's try this same example again, but show you other ways they can do it. What if the options were as follows?

A. I, IV
B. I, III
C. II
D. III, IV

By following The Process, we would still be *sure* Option 1 is a wrong answer. I have not suddenly developed a strong fondness for raw fish. By continuing to Step 2 of The Process we would go *straight to the bottom* where we would eliminate Options A and B because they both have an I in them. Remember, we would not have read choices III and IV *yet* to know I like them. We just know that since we are sure about 1, that guarantees that both Options A and B are both wrong. *Draw a line through them.*

Next, we would proceed to Step 3, to compare and contrast the remaining options. In this case, those options would be C and D. By comparing and contrasting C and D, we quickly see they have nothing in common! This means that I either like II (broccoli) more than *both* Italian food and chocolate (highly unlikely) or vice versa. Now, let's be honest. We are all into health and fitness these days. But, come on. Who do you know that truthfully loves broccoli more than Italian food and chocolate? It's just not happening.

Therefore, based on comparing and contrasting Options C and D, we select D as the correct answer. Bingo! Another multiple-multiple bites the dust!

One last thing about the multiple-multiples: Sometimes the test developers are just plain kind to us. What if the choices had looked like this?

A. I, IV
B. I, III
C. I, II
D. III, IV

This one would be one that would make us all fall to our knees in worship. In Step 1 of The Process we would eliminate the whole sushi thing, choice I. In Step 2, we would go straight to the bottom where we would see, wonder of wonders, there is an I in Options A, B, and C! That means that, technically, without even reading Option D, by *process of elimination* we know it *must* be the answer! Upon reading Option D, we love it! It has both Italian food and chocolate! In other words, this one is just plain old *easy.* Believe it or not, there actually will be some questions on the test that are this obvious . . . if you are staying calm, cool, collected, confident, and almost downright cocky. If you are all stressed out, not following The Process, or ignoring The Dot Game after I told you over and over to use it to help you manage the clock and your anxiety, *you will not recognize these easy ones.* So, be alert, follow my suggestions, mark these easy ones, move one, and be happy. They are not trick questions. They are gifts.

Needless to say, many questions will not be this obvious. They will be less factual and will require application of decision making based on the ten learner-centered leadership competencies. Still, you should *follow the same process.*

Multiple-multiples can turn out to be your best friend if you will follow this process. Students repeatedly tell me that by following this method they begin to wish *all* the questions on the test were multiple-multiples. Turn a potentially frightening situation into a positive one by following the fantastic Elaine Wilmore Process.

KEY WORDS AND THEMES: "SHERRYS" REVISITED

Review Chapters 3 through 12 on the learner-centered competencies. You do not need to memorize them. However, read them over and over, slowly, for comprehension and synthesis of their concepts. Think about what they mean. Practice visualizing how you will put them into practice when you pass this test and become a superintendent. Go back and review Chapter 2, It's All Good, particularly focusing on the discussion on important recurring concepts and themes as presented in Figure 2.2. You will see key words and concepts repeated such as multiple uses of data for a concept and *all* and *facilitate* as words. Sometimes you will even see answer choices that appear to almost *quote* a competency. When you see answer choices that utilize the same words or concepts, pick that answer. If the test developers had liked other concepts, language, or words better, they would have used them. Stick with ideas you *know* they like. That is why they are in the competencies!

THE IDEAL SUPERINTENDENT

Let's review the concept of the Ideal Superintendent. The Ideal Superintendent always does what is right, even when it is difficult or politically unpopular. Think "ideal," then mark the ideal response. Collaborate with everyone on everything. Facilitate and align all students, teachers, parents, and everyone else for maximum productivity and efficiency to ensure continuous student success. You are the Ideal Superintendent. You are on a relentless pursuit of excellence for all district and community stakeholders. If all else fails, think, "Which one of these crazy choices would Elaine put?" Then mark it because it *is the right answer!*

STRATEGY SUMMARY

The Dot Game is a strategy to help you utilize your time effectively while also keeping your anxiety level down and confidence up. Use it. Repeat it till you have completed the test. However, if you have gone through the test two to three times and still have dots left, mark the responses you think the Ideal Superintendent would do. Remember, this test is not designed for what the average, run-of-the-mill superintendent would do. It is built on a philosophy that all superintendents want to do the *right, moral,* and *ethical* things necessary to produce districts that maximize student learning productivity and character for an improved democratic society. Do *not* select answers that you think are what is actually done in districts if there is a *better* choice that reaches to a higher standard of moral or ethical responsibility to the district community.

By playing The Dot Game and The Dog and Star Game as well as always thinking "ideal," you will make good choices and pass the TExES exam ASAP. Once you pass it, get your certification, and land a great job leading a district, remember that it is your moral and ethical responsibility to do the right thing even when something else would be easier. Live the competencies. Let your walk match your talk for the benefit of every student. We are not in leadership for a quick or easy fix. We are in it to have a real impact on our world, to leave a legacy of unparalleled excellence, and to know when we go to bed at night that we have done every single thing we can to make those things happen. There has never been a time in the past when you have been needed more. Go forth, and do well. I believe in you, so always remember me, how I have advised you, and, please, keep me updated on all the wonderful things you are going to accomplish.

Creating a Personal Success Plan

You have goals of passing the TExES examination, obtaining superintendent certification, and becoming a great district leader focused on improving student performance. The first step in achieving these goals is passing this test. You have the necessary knowledge base from successful completion of your university or alternative preparation program. Upon reading, analyzing, and truly incorporating the concepts presented in this book into your leadership style, you will also have a solid understanding of the theoretical framework around which the test is constructed. Each part of the exam, whether the multiple-choice or data analysis sections, has been written to measure your understanding and capability of applying the ten superintendent learner-centered competencies fully detailed in Chapters 3 through 12. Section III has also provided you with specific strategies to help you make correct decisions regarding scenarios on the exam. What else can you do to assure you pass?

Two of Stephen Covey's *The 7 Habits of Highly Effective People* (1990) are

- begin with the end in mind, and
- sharpen the saw.

In preparing for what could possibly be the most important exam of your career, you need to do both. But, in simple language, what do these two habits mean, and how can you apply them in creating a personal plan for success on the superintendent TExES exam?

First, to begin with the end in mind means looking ahead to where you want to be (i.e., passing the TExES exam), then strategically calculating the exact things you must do between now and then to achieve it. Goals without deadlines are only dreams. Because of that, you must set a specific deadline for each thing you hope to accomplish in test preparation. Waiting to the last minute will not get you where you want to be. You will either run out of time before the test or end up in such a frenzied state that it will be increasingly difficult to make prudent choices of answers to questions and data analysis.

Similarly, as you reflectively and insightfully consider the exact things you need to do while preparing for the exam, you also will be sharpening the saw. Covey (1990) gives the analogy of lumberjacks in a contest to see who can chop the most trees. One lumberjack immediately starts chopping. Another takes his time and spends several important minutes calmly sharpening the blade on his saw. Bystanders likely thought he had not picked a fine time to take up saw sharpening.

However, once this lumberjack was convinced his blade was ready, he began to saw on a tree. Because his saw was sharper than the other fellow's, he was more efficient and effective cutting down the trees. He subsequently won the contest. The point is once we look ahead to what we need to accomplish before the exam, once we begin now (our test preparation planning process) with the end in mind (actually passing the exam), we must also analyze, procure, and implement the best tools and resources available to help us sharpen our saws to maximize their utilization.

Taking these things into consideration, stop now and seriously consider the following. Aside from my superintendent preparation program and this wonderful book,

- What other exact resources would be beneficial in helping you understand and best be able to apply the ten superintendent competencies?
- Who can you talk to, or consult with? Who has the knowledge, expertise, and wisdom to best help you understand and be able to apply the competencies in scenario-based problem solving?
- Who can you talk to, or consult with, who can share helpful organizational techniques that can benefit you in the data analysis section of the exam?
- Who can you talk to, or consult with, to help you with time and stress management as you prepare for the test?
- Who can you talk to, or consult with, to help you create and implement your own personal success plan?

- Once developed and implemented, what modification and account-ability mechanisms can you utilize to enhance the plan and hold you responsible for following it?

Each of these is a serious question. There are no absolutely right or wrong answers. They will vary from test taker to test taker and situation to situation. Figure 15.1 below shows a sample template to help you organize your planning process. Whether you use it, or something different, use something. Write it down. Include a timeline and accountability system. Remember, in the end, wanting to pass the TExES exam is only a dream if you do not have a plan with a responsible timeline and account-ability process.

Figure 15.1 Personal Success Plan Template

Thing, idea, or project to address	Resources I will need to accomplish this thing, idea, or project	Projected date to have everything ready to begin doing this thing, idea, or project	Projected date to complete this thing, idea, or project	Evaluation: How will I be able to measure what I have learned through this thing, idea, or project?	Accountability: Who, what, or how will I be held accountable for accomplishing this thing, idea, or project?

TIPS FOR THOSE WHO HAVE NOT BEEN SUCCESSFUL ON THE EXAM . . . YET

For various reasons, sometimes a person will not immediately pass the test. Health, family, and stress issues are some reasons people do not pass. Because the test is long and involves a lot of reading, test takers who are slow readers, or who have poor reading comprehension skills, sometimes have difficulty. But the major reason people do not immediately pass is a lack of proper understanding of the ten learner-centered competencies. If you fall in any of these categories, do not be discouraged. This is the longest and most reading-intensive TExES exam that currently exists. Developing and using a personal success plan such as the template pro-vided in Figure 15.1 helps you to be able to create a concrete schema to help you succeed. Thus, the real issue becomes identifying the specific things you can do to improve your scores. If you did not do well last time, study your scores. Is there a domain in which you came very close to passing? If so, what are the things you can do to focus and improve in this area? The same is true for your lowest domain. Really focus on this area because it is dragging you down. Your lowest domain is your highest area of need. If you do not have much time to prepare, concentrate your attention on the chapters of this book that address your lowest area. Seek solid ways to increase your knowledge base and application skills in this area. Do not be afraid to ask district administrators to help you. Most of them will want to help you, but they need guidance on how to do it. If you can share with them your greatest areas of need, they can center their mentoring efforts in those areas.

THE "ELAINE WILMORE 5-C PLAN"

If you have truly studied, synthesized, and internalized the leadership concepts presented in this book, created and utilized a personal success plan, and sought assistance and mentoring in targeted areas from people you respect, you should do quite well this time. However, there are some additional things you can do to improve both your likelihood and confidence. You need the benefit of the "Elaine Wilmore 5-C Plan." The 5-C Plan consists of going into this test:

Calm,

Cool,

Collected,

Confident, and almost downright . . .

Cocky.

I have had *numerous* people from around the state say that prior to attending my preparation classes or reading my books, they had been unsuccessful in passing the principal or superintendent TExES exam. Yet after *doing what I have stressed to them to do*, they have passed their test. Hearing this kind of news never fails but to make me happy. Actually, this kind of news, particularly from someone who had yet to be successful on one of the tests, really makes me smile from the inside out. Like everyone else, I am human. I get tired (real tired, actually), and even I can get worn down from the stress of life. Hearing from people who pass the test, hearing the joy in their voices, cards, letters, and e-mails lifts me up more than you can ever know. Your success is important to me. I want you to pass this test. I want you to become the best superintendents our state and others have ever seen. Our kids deserve nothing less. Therefore, we have got to work together to get you through this test!

Here are some specific suggestions to help you do exactly that:

- Application of Competencies: Go back to each of the ten learner-centered competencies. Read, study, and analyze them slowly for comprehension, not memorization, of the concepts they represent. Remember, the key here is *comprehension* of the concepts, not memorizing them.

    o To help you comprehend and be able to apply their *meaning*, develop a portfolio with ten sections. There should be one section for each of the ten competencies. Begin watching district-level administrators around you in various contexts. In your mind, try to associate every positive thing they do with at least one of the competencies. Take notes, collect artifacts, and write brief reflective summaries of each activity. Place the notes into the appropriate section of your competency portfolio. There is something about framing thoughts into logical sentences that helps us more fully understand what they mean. Otherwise, what could we write down? Writing the brief summaries will thus help you analyze the activity you have observed into its various components.

    o Often you will have difficulty deciding if an activity belongs with one or a different competency. That is all right. It probably does go both places. Do not stress over this. The superintendent's job is an integrated position. We are not going to split hairs over what goes where. You will not receive bonus points on the test for knowing exactly which questions go with which competencies. *The important thing is that you are connecting real life applications with the concepts of the competencies.* You are thus making the competencies come alive. You are internalizing and synthesizing them. When you see scenarios of superintendent behavior in the TExES questions or the data analysis section, you will already be accustomed to analyzing behaviors and making prudent organizational decisions. Your portfolio will help you select the appropriate responses. Your portfolio will be personal, authentic, and applied TExES preparation.

Having someone with whom to do these activities collaboratively will multiply the benefits for both you and them. If you have an encouraging mentor, supportive friends, or even a friendly classmate, ask them if once a week they will take the time to sit down and let you walk through your portfolio with them. It will be particularly beneficial if your partner is preparing for the test too. You can share your ideas, thoughts, and portfolios with each other, which will multiply the rewards. Orally describe each artifact, set of notes, and so forth, and then summarize how they apply to this competency and what you learned from them. The act of orally describing what something is and why you selected it will manifest itself in critical and reflective thinking. These are, of course, higher order thinking skills, which is exactly what this test is all about. Benjamin Bloom would be proud. So will you when you get your passing TExES scores!

- Content: Look at the score sheet or sheets you have received in previous TExES endeavors. Write down your scores *per domain* rather than your total score. Forget your total score. If you bring up your domain and competency scores, your domain and competency scores will automatically bring up your overall score.

  o Within your scores, you will have relative strengths, which are your higher scores. You will also have relative weaknesses, which are your lower scores. Target the areas you would like to focus on for this test administration. Go back to your college textbooks and notes for those areas. Review them. Study particularly the corresponding chapters of this book that go with those competencies. Study the additional resources that I have suggested per competency. In this way, your preparation will be focused on your greatest needs. You will be working *smarter* rather than harder.

  o Reading Comprehension or Speed Reading Courses or Review: I am convinced there are many highly intelligent people who have had difficulty passing various TExES exams due to a combination of factors. Some are not prepared cognitively. They do not have the appropriate knowledge base. Others have, amazingly, never had the *philosophy* of learner-centered leadership stressed to them. How can anyone be expected to pass a test if they do not have a comprehension of the theoretical framework on which it is built? Others are lacking in language and test-taking skills.

    Some, though, have difficulty with TExES due to the intense amount of reading involved. Every decision set and question involves reading, comprehension, analysis, and synthesis for application. Although many of these people are smart and successful in life, reading comprehension is not high on their talent lists. Sometimes comprehension is not the only problem. Sometimes they read very slowly. Some are also slowed down because English is not their first language. It takes time to read in English, process and possibly translate what has been read into their primary language, then convert everything back to English to pick a correct response. All of this takes time and time is not your friend. *I am your friend!* Do what I tell you to do! If you don't play the game my way, the clock could win instead of you. Once you start having to fight the clock, we're in trouble. Eventually, you may begin to panic. *We know for a fact that panic is counterproductive in passing the TExES exam and virtually any other high-stakes test.* When anxiety goes up, productivity goes down. That is not what we want. We want productivity to stay up and anxiety to stay down. Practice deep breathing or yoga relaxation techniques. I've never learned yoga, but I delivered three large babies by natural childbirth, thanks to the help of Lamaze breathing techniques. Believe me, those same Lamaze breathing techniques have served me quite well through the years when I have been stressed. In short, do whatever works to keep you calm as long as it is legal and moral.

If reading comprehension or speed is an issue with you, you already know it. There are various places, including Sylvan Learning Centers and university or school district continuing education courses, that offer classes in these areas. Another good resource would be local English, language arts, or reading teachers. They often know of many good books, tapes, or techniques that would be beneficial. Your public library, as well as school and university libraries, also will have resources to assist you. I cannot stress enough the importance of reading comprehension in passing this test. If you think you read well, but have been unsuccessful in passing the TExES exam more than once, what on earth do you stand to lose by seeking to improve your reading skills? Not only will it help you pass this test, it will also improve your quality of life in countless other areas.

TIPS FOR OUT-OF-STATE FUTURE TEXAS SUPERINTENDENTS

Very often, there are people from out of state, particularly practicing administrators, who seek to become superintendents in Texas. Welcome! We love our great state, and welcome you to it. Be sure you bring along a firm commitment to learner-centered leadership and to improving student performance because that's what education in Texas is all about.

The competency information provided in this book will bring things you have known for years to the forefront of your mind. To my surprise, many of the states adjacent to Texas are not stressing learner-centered leadership. Or it could be that they are, but you have been out of school for a long time and not actively involved in this type professional development. We can solve that.

It is particularly important for you to think "Ideal Superintendent." In many ways, it is more important for you than it is for the nonsuperintendents taking the test. Remember, this test is designed for *entry-level* administrative skills. If you have years of experience, you will have a tendency to look at potential responses from an experienced perspective. You know what will or will not work in real life.

Forget real life. Think *ideal.* If a response may seem a little *unrealistic* to you, but you know that in an *ideal school* with an *ideal superintendent* that is likely what would happen, *mark that answer!* It is the right one! The idea here is to lift the benchmark of superintendent behavior as much as possible, especially with new superintendents, to the level of ideal. Remember our pal Les Brown again. Aim for the moon. Even if you miss it, you will land among the stars. We want *every* superintendent, new and experienced, to aim for the moon, the very epitome of the ideal superintendent, every day in every way. In so doing, our schools may not reach the top, but they sure will achieve higher than they currently are. What on earth could be wrong with that?

The last thing I suggest is for you to get on the Internet and study different Academic Excellence Indicator System (AEIS) and Adequate Yearly Progress (AYP) reports for various schools and districts. Since AEIS reports are a Texas thing, you may not be familiar with their layout. But you will be familiar with the types of data presented therein. Look up an AEIS report and play with it. Assess them for the good, the bad, and the ugly. Design interventions that could potentially improve student learning. Becoming familiar and comfortable with AEIS and AYP reports prior to testing will save you time and anxiety on the day you test. You will be able to whiz right through it, playing The Dot Game, of course. Remember: *Think ideal.*

EVERYONE, TEXANS AND NON-TEXANS ALIKE

What else should you do to prepare yourself cognitively, psychologically, and emotionally?

Mantras

The administrative TExES exams are mind games based on implementing student-centered leadership. The domains and competencies develop and portray this philosophy. In this book, you have studied, processed, and applied them in every conceivable scenario. Cognitively you are prepared. Logically, you should and will pass the test.

What about illogically? What if you are so frightened that you cannot think straight? What if, deep down, you are truly scared you will fail the test? What if your job or future job depends on passing? You cannot think about being an Ideal Superintendent or developing an Ideal District because you are too busy breaking out in hives.

You've got to break that paradigm. Your mind is the front wheel of the wheelbarrow that drives your life. Your mind must be convinced you will not just pass TExES, you will ace it. You will knock it dead. You will do so well that they will audit your results. You will do great! You will make me proud! Frankly, you will simply be amazing! People will look at you in awe!

To convince your inner self of that, begin at this moment saying out loud, "I am going to ace this test. I am going to do great. I am thinking 'ideal' all day long." Do these a hundred times a day from now until you pass. Write it on fifty Post-it Notes and put them everywhere. Each time you see one, read it out loud. Say it with spirit. Practice being calm, cool, collected, confident, and almost downright cocky! Repeat the mantra until you, and everyone around you, is sick of hearing it. Repeat it alone, in public, in boring meetings, in your car, while exercising or shopping. Sing it in the shower really loud. Repeat it till you drive yourself and others crazy. Repeat it over and over as you get ready and drive to the test. Keep repeating it as you take the test. You are what you believe you are. You are a success. You are going to make a real difference in this world. Believe it. Do it. You will be great!

FROM NOW TILL THE WEEK YOU TEST

From now till the test, review Section II of this book regularly. Put that in your personal success plan. Study the competencies. Read through them slowly as you focus on the concepts they represent. Do not attempt to memorize anything, but do focus on the terms, language, and common themes that emerge. Once a week, review Chapters 3 through 12. I do *not* want you to think, "Well, I read the book, so I am ready for the test." That is real nice, and you may pass the test. But you also need to prepare, integrate, synthesize, apply, and *not forget* all I have been preaching to you about these competencies.

By synthesizing the competencies over and over until you are sick of them and never want to see them again, you will become as familiar and comfortable with them and the concepts they represent as you currently are with driving to school. Driving to school may not be a big deal to you because you do it every day. But remember when you were first learning to drive? Driving *anywhere* was a big deal. You watched every corner, every traffic light, and likely gripped the steering wheel tightly when other cars came your way.

Think of these competencies as learning to drive. I want you so thoroughly familiar and comfortable with them that when you take the TExES, they will seem as natural as driving to school. You are the driver of this test. Drive it well.

THE WEEK YOU TEST

You have faithfully prepared. You have read Section II at least once a week until the week of the test. It is now time to get more intense. Reread the entire book. Focus this time on Section III with its strategies and techniques for success. Then *each night* before you go to bed, read through the competencies *again*. Do it as the last thing before you turn off the lights. Research says the last thing you have on your mind before falling asleep stays in your mind all night long. That is exactly where we want this information to be. We want it working its way through your mind while you sleep, eat, work, bathe, or fall into a coma.

As before, read for comprehension, not memorization. By reading the competencies many times, key words and phrases that appear on the test, especially in answers, will jump right out at you as if they were in bold print. That is good. Those are *stars*. Mark them. We know if the test developers had liked other words or phrases better, they would have used them. When they use their own language, they are *giving* you the answer. Take them up on it and say, "Oh! Thank you!"

Then send me chocolate, plain with no nuts, as a thank-you for clueing you in on all this. I don't like nuts in my chocolate because we already have way too many nuts in education. I also really like pink roses, just in case you wanted to know. There are no nuts in roses.

WHAT TO DO, AND NOT DO, THE NIGHT BEFORE THE TEST

The night before the test is similar to the last minutes of the test if you are still sitting there. If you are not familiar with the competencies and test-taking strategies presented here by that point, it is not going to come to you by osmosis or divine intervention. However, I have had more than one student promise me that prayer works. I am a big believer in prayer myself.

I pray for all my students before they test. Maybe that is why they do so well. From this point on, consider yourself my student.

In truth, this is what I want you to do. You will test on a Saturday. On the Friday before you test, come home from school or wherever and *relax*. Go out to dinner. Take in a movie that is *light* and fun with pure, mindless drivel. Do *not* go see anything stressful. You have enough stress in your life right now. You can see intense or stressful movies after the test when you are so relieved to have it behind you that you know that you could single-handedly slay dragons. Think of it as a victory march.

But the night before the test, you want mindless drivel. You want *absolutely nothing stressful* going on. Talk to your family, assuming you have one, ahead of time. Make sure they understand the *importance* of you having a calm night. If the cat has kittens, let someone else tend to it. As far as I am concerned, I do not even want you to *know about it.* And if you win the Publisher's Clearinghouse, don't let anyone tell you until *after* this blasted test. Otherwise, it would be a distraction for you to think about how you are going to spend, invest, or give away all that money. After the test, you can celebrate and, of course, invite me.

On the night before the test, relax. Go out to dinner some place you like. Do something fun. Come home early. Take a nice, hot bubble bath, preferably with *peach* bubbles, in my honor, of course. Men, just take the bubble bath and shut up. Your wives will love it! You will become very relaxed, which is exactly my purpose for you.

Then go to bed. You may read through the competencies one last time. If you do not know them by now, cramming will not help. Read through them, turn off the lights, and say your prayers. The party is over.

WHAT TO DO, AND NOT DO, THE MORNING OF THE TEST

Set your clock to get up in plenty of time, particularly if you are assigned a morning testing. I do not want you rushed and messing up all that good relaxation from last night. Have *plenty of time* to get ready and arrive. If necessary, get directions and practice driving the route to the testing site. Don't be late!

Eat something. Even if you are not a breakfast person, eat something anyway. Research shows people who have something in their stomachs to fuel their bodies perform better. We want you to have *peak performance.* This is Olympics Day for you. Don't you know all those athletes have specially designed meals to ensure peak performance? This is your Olympics. You may not have a nutritionist at your house, but you do have something loaded with protein. Avoid carbohydrates this morning. They may give you a quick rush, but by midmorning, your blood sugar will crash. Testing day is not the day for your blood sugar to crash. Eat protein instead. After the test, you can pig out on as many carbs as you want, but not now!

Dress comfortably and in layers. This may be the only time in your life that looking good does not count. Wear something comfortable. This includes your shoes. You do not need aching feet during the TExES examination. If you decide your feet hurt during the test, shed the shoes. If your feet tend to get cold when you are nervous, bring extra socks. Dress in layers. I have had *multiple* students around the entire state complain that the testing sites are really cold. If you dress in layers, you can shed some of them if you get too warm. There is nothing worse than being cold during a test. From the other perspective, some people respond to stress by getting really hot and sweating. Others respond by their blood pressure slowing down instead of going up. They get cold. By dressing in layers, you will be prepared for any situation. And, last, if you have a lucky charm or talisman, wear it.

Arrive at the test site early. You do not want to be rushed or to take any chances with traffic, wrecks, emergencies, nuclear attack, and so on. There will be a large number of other test takers at your testing site. Most of them will *not* be taking the same test as you. The lengths of different tests vary, so do not be surprised or chagrined if people sitting around you get up and leave before you are anywhere close to being through. Do not assume that they are innately brilliant and that you are a bump on a pickle. That is not true. *You* are the one that is innately brilliant and *fabulously* well prepared. They may be taking a different test. Or they have guessed their way all the way through our test and are hoping for a computer miracle during grading. *You* stay focused on taking care of your own business. Do not worry about theirs.

Make sure you remember to play The Dot Game. It is such a simple strategy that you may be tempted to not do it. Do it anyway. It will save you both time and grief. It is a very, very good test-taking strategy to maximize your productivity. Both your body and your mind need this structure for addressing confusing questions. Review everything about The Dot Game the week of the test. Apply what you know. It is a well-seasoned game and has greater validity than the lottery. Utilize the Dog and Star Game. Work your way through the test two to three times using both strategies. Then hang it up. Remember, you do not have to make 100% on this test. All you have to do is pass it. Speaking as someone who has spent nine glorious years serving on a public school board, I can assure you that boards do not utilize TExES exam scores when selecting district administrators. You are well prepared for this test. You have answered every question. You have given it your all. You are done. Go home!

LIVING YOUR LIFE AFTER THE TEST

Celebrate!!!! Although most people think that they leave the testing site brain dead simply due to the length of the test, you will also know in your heart that you passed this test. You will have a deep sense of accomplishment. You will feel an even greater sense of accomplishment the day you get your scores. But, until then, there is not one more thing you can do except celebrate. You deserve it. If you want to see an action thriller tonight, go do it. If you want to run the Boston Marathon, go do it. If you want to eat your weight in chocolate, invite me. But whatever you do, do it because it is something that fills your soul with joy. You have accomplished a major goal. You have taken and passed the superintendent TExES exam. You may not have your scores yet, but you know something that the computer does not. *You won!*

Go forth and make every day of your life all it can be for yourself and others. Do something kind for a stranger. Make a difference in the life of at least one person every day. Change the world, one district at a time. Yes, I do realize that this sounds like a Pollyanna way to approach life and educational leadership. But our world has enough negativity and ugliness in it. We have terrorists, wars, poverty, hunger, abuse, disease, lack of respect for others with different opinions and perspectives; the list goes on and on. We are surrounded by it.

Let's be different. Let's do everything we can to fill the world with joy. Idealistic? Yes. Impossible? No, not if you will help me.

Will you come along?

SECTION IV

After You
Pass the Test

16

That's What I'm Talking About

ACTUALLY BECOMING CERTIFIED

Once you receive your passing scores in the mail, you can shout for joy, jump up and down, call your entire family and friends, toss young children in the air, shout the news to strangers on the street, *send me roses and chocolate*, and be quite proud of yourself. You have accomplished a very great thing! I can already tell you just how proud I am of you. Now, don't let me down! You must go out there and be the ideal superintendent that you have proven that you know how to be. I am counting on you to do exactly that.

However, after the celebrating, there are a few things left for you to do to actually obtain your superintendent certification. It is your responsibility to officially apply for your certificate with the State Board for Educator Certification (SBEC) at www.sbec.state.tx.us. There will be a certification fee, which you will pay directly to them.

Your university, or alternative preparation program, will already have received your scores from the State. *After* you have gone to the SBEC Web site, applied for your certificate, and paid your fee, you should contact the certification office at your university or alternative preparation program. Their endorsement of your application is required. However, they cannot go online to approve your application if you have not applied for it. That's why you must do the online application through SBEC *before* contacting your certification officer. Do not forget the order of these important steps. Without doing them, you will not become certified regardless of how many tests you ace. Many, but not all, universities and alternative programs will charge you a small processing fee for completing your certification paperwork. To avoid confusion, remember that this is a different fee from the one you paid SBEC for your actual certification.

If you are an out-of-state test taker and not directly affiliated with any Texas university or approved alternative provider, you will need to contact SBEC directly regarding your certification paperwork.

During the time that it takes SBEC to process your paperwork, you are not yet officially certified. However, you are "certifiable." This means you *are* eligible to be employed as a certified superintendent. The school district may require you to present evidence that you have completed all program requirements including passing your TExES exam. This is something your university will be pleased to provide. Usually, a simple letter on official university (or alternative program) letterhead stating your status will suffice. Certifications are now provided online so both you and your district can see when your actual certification is finalized. It is a wonderful thing when you see your certification appear by your name online. Print it out, and show it off to everyone you see. Tell them how hard you worked to get that piece of paper and how much you *really* love me for helping you get it. It's your job to make me famous, but that won't be on the TExES exam.

ACE IT!

With today's critical shortage of certified administrators, you could very well be hired as a superintendent before your certification becomes official. In fact, it is entirely possible that you could be hired before you even take the test. Regardless, you still must take the test. Having the job before you are certified does not exempt you from taking and passing the TExES exam. If that happens to you, do not blow off the test. It is still very serious to your career. Make sure you still study, prepare, and do every single thing I have told you to do to pass this test.

In the end, certification is more than a necessary step to your long-term employment as a district superintendent. Meeting all certification requirements through course work, practicums or internships, and the TExES examination are all designed for one purpose. *That purpose is to help you be the best superintendent on the face of this earth.* Nothing less will do. Is it a competition to be the best superintendent? Of course it's not. We want every district and every school to be absolutely outstanding. We want every teacher to be able to teach where each student can and will learn. We want every student to graduate equipped for success in life regardless if that means entering the world of work, the military, or higher education. We want every graduate to be an informed, voting citizen within a literate, free, and democratic society.

Until all of this happens, we are not through with our work. We have not reached our destination where all schools and all of society are ideal. Early in this book, I told you that I am the Pollyanna of School Leadership. I reminded you that we already have enough educational cynics and do not need any more. Stretching toward the ideal may, or may not, be realistic. But it is absolutely necessary that you aim for it. If we don't aim for ideal, how will we ever make significant strides toward reaching it? Your part in this is to be the best superintendent your district, town, the Great State of Texas, and the world have ever seen. That is what it will take to change, to improve, and to enhance our global society, one school and district at a time. Let's start now with you.

Will it be a daunting task? Yes, it will. Will you become tired, frustrated, and totally disgusted with complicated, complex community, district, state, and federal politics? Yes, at times you will. But will this also be the most challenging and personally rewarding job you could ever imagine? Without a doubt it will be. There will be tears of fatigue and frustration, but there will also be tears of joy and elation. There will be times you want to beat your head against a wall or prefer to beat a few other people's heads instead. Yet there will also be times of jumping up and down internally and externally over something magnificent that has happened, something that those with lesser faith believed could not be done. Yet you knew that it could. They were the cynics while you were the idealist. You knew that good things *would* happen because there is nothing on this earth that can make you give up in your continuing quest to change the world one school and district at a time.

You have now passed the TExES examination and are headed into your future with anticipation, hope, joy, courage, perseverance, and a little bit of fear. May every day of your journey to do what is right, to do what is ideal, to stay proactive, positive, and persuasive be the best day imaginable. It is all before you now. Just reach out and take it. You've worked for it. You've earned it. It's yours. Just remember to send me the chocolate and roses.

May you be blessed. Go forth and make me proud. Make the world a better place. Together we *can* be the difference. Will you join me as we try?

Now, let's do it! *Ace that test!*

Always for the Future,
Your friend and mentor now and forever,
The Proud Pollyanna of District and School Leadership,
Elaine L. Wilmore, PhD
Eternally grateful to be the daughter of my parents,
the late Lee and Irene Litchfield of Port Arthur, Texas

Suggested Additional Reading

This list is not intended to be an exhaustive guide, but a source for supplemental reading that supports the concepts presented in the Superintendent TExES Exam. Many of these resources include content that is relevant to more than one domain.

DOMAIN 1

Abrams, J. (2009). *Having hard conversations.* Thousand Oaks, CA: Corwin.

Bennis, W. (1989). *Why leaders can't lead.* San Francisco: Jossey-Bass.

Bates, D., Durka, G., & Schweitzer, F. (2006). *Education, religion and society: Essays in honour of John M. Hull.* New York: Routledge.

Batey, C. S. (1996). *Parents are lifesavers: A handbook for parent involvement in schools.* Thousand Oaks, CA: Corwin.

Beaudoin, M. N., & Taylor, M. (2004). *Creating a positive school culture: How principals and teachers can solve problems together.* Thousand Oaks, CA: Corwin.

Bell, L., & Stevenson, H. (2006). *Education policy: Process, themes and impact.* New York: Routledge.

Bennis, W. (1999). *Old dogs, new tricks.* Provo, UT: Executive Excellence.

BenShea, N. (2000). *What every principal would like to say . . . and what to say next time.* Thousand Oaks, CA: Corwin.

Blair-Stanford, N., & Dickmann, M. H. (2002). *Connecting leadership to the brain.* Thousand Oaks, CA: Corwin.

Blanchard, K., & Bowles, S. (1998). *Gung-ho!* New York: William Morrow.

Blanchard, K., Hybels, B., & Hodges, P. (1999). *Leadership by the book: Tools to transform your workplace.* New York: William Morrow.

Blanchard, K., Oncken, W., Jr., & Burrows, H. (1989). *The one minute manager meets the monkey.* New York: William Morrow.

Blanchard, K., & Peale, N. V. (1988). *The power of ethical management.* New York: William Morrow.

Blanchard, K., Zigarmi, P., & Zigmari, D. (1985). *Leadership and the one minute manager.* New York: William Morrow.

Bolman, L. G., & Deal, T. E. (1997). *Reframing organizations: Artistry, choice and leadership* (2nd ed.). San Francisco: Jossey-Bass.

Bolman, L. G., & Deal, T. E. (2001). *Leading with soul: An uncommon journey of spirit.* San Francisco: Jossey-Bass.

Bolman, L. G., & Deal, T. E. (2002). *Reframing the path to school leadership: A guide for teachers and principals.* Thousand Oaks, CA: Corwin.

Brock, B. L., & Grady, M. L. (2000). *Rekindling the flame.* Thousand Oaks, CA: Corwin.

Brower, R. E., & Balch, B. V. (2005). *Transformational leadership & decision making in schools.* Thousand Oaks, CA: Corwin.

Brubaker, D. L. (2006). *The charismatic leader: The presentation of self and the creation of educational settings.* Thousand Oaks, CA: Corwin.

Burke, M. A., & Picus, L. O. (2001). *Developing community-empowered schools.* Thousand Oaks, CA: Corwin.

Capasso, R. L., & Daresh, J. C. (2001). *The school administrator internship handbook: Leading, mentoring, and participating in the internship program.* Thousand Oaks, CA: Corwin.

Chadwick, K. G. (2004). *Improving schools through community engagement: A practical guide for educators.* Thousand Oaks, CA: Corwin.

Cherry, D., & Spiegel, J. (2006). *Leadership, myth, & metaphor: Finding common ground to guide effective school change.* Thousand Oaks, CA: Corwin.

Covey, S. R. (1990). *Principle-centered leadership.* New York: Simon & Schuster.

Covey, S. R., Merrill, A. R., & Merrill, R. R. (1994). *First things first.* New York: Simon & Schuster.

Datnow, A., & Murphy, J. F. (2002). *Leadership lessons from comprehensive school reforms.* Thousand Oaks, CA: Corwin.

Davies, B., & Brighouse, T. (2009). *Passionate leadership in education.* Thousand Oaks, CA: Corwin.

Decker, R. H. (1997). *When a crisis hits: Will your school be ready?* Thousand Oaks, CA: Corwin.

DePree, M. (1989). *Leadership is an art.* New York: Dell.

DePree, M. (1997). *Leading without power: Finding hope in serving community.* San Francisco: Jossey-Bass.

DeWitt Wallace-Reader's Digest Fund Study Conference. (1992). *Developing a framework for the continual professional development of administrators in the northeast.* Andover, MA: Regional Laboratory for Educational Improvement of the Northeast & Islands. (ERIC Document Reproduction Service No. ED383104)

Doyle, D. P., & Pimentel, S. (1999). *Raising the standard: An eight-step action guide for schools and communities.* Thousand Oaks, CA: Corwin.

Drucker Foundation. (1996). *The leader of the future.* San Francisco: Jossey-Bass.

Duncan, S. F., & Goddard, H. W. (2005). *Family life education: Principles and practices for effective outreach.* Thousand Oaks, CA: Sage Publications.

Dunklee, D. R. (2000). *If you want to lead, not just manage: A primer for principals.* Thousand Oaks, CA: Corwin.

Dunklee, D. R., & Shoop, R. J. (2001). *The principal's quick-reference guide to school law: reducing liability, litigation, and other potential legal tangles.* Thousand Oaks: Corwin.

Dyer, K. M. (2000). *The intuitive principal.* Thousand Oaks, CA: Corwin.

Earl, L. M., & Katz, S. (2006). *Leading schools in a data-rich world: Harnessing data for school improvement.* Thousand Oaks, CA: Corwin.

Eisner, E. W. (2005). *Reimagining schools: The selected works of Elliot W. Eisner.* New York: Routledge.

Elias, M., Arnold, H., & Steiger Hussey, C. (Eds.). (2002). *EQ + IQ = best leadership practices for caring.* Thousand Oaks, CA: Corwin.

English, F. W. (1994). *Theory in educational administration.* New York: HarperCollins.

Epstein, J. L., Sanders, M. G., Sheldon, S. B., Simon, B. S., Salinas, K. C., Jansorn, N. R., et al. (2009). *School, family, and community partnerships: Your handbook for action* (3rd ed.). Thousand Oaks, CA: Corwin.

Erickson, C. L., Morley, R. E., & Veale, J. R. (2002). *Practical evaluations for collaborative services.* Thousand Oaks, CA: Corwin.

Feinberg, W. (2006). *For goodness sake: Religious schools and education for democratic citizenry.* New York: Routledge.

Fiore, D. J., & Whitaker, T. (2001). *Dealing with difficult parents (and with parents in difficult situations).* Larchmont, NY: Eye on Education.

Fullan, M. (2001). *Leading in a culture of change.* San Francisco: Jossey-Bass.

Fullan, M. (2003). *The moral imperative of school leadership.* Thousand Oaks, CA: Corwin.

Fullan, M. (2005). *Leadership & sustainability: System thinkers in action.* Thousand Oaks, CA: Corwin.

Giancola, J. M., Hutchinson, J. K. (2005). *Transforming the culture of school leadership: Humanizing our practice.* Thousand Oaks, CA: Corwin.

Glaser, J. (2005). *Leading through collaboration: Guiding groups to productive solutions.* Thousand Oaks, CA: Corwin.

Goldring, E., & Berends, M. (2009). *Leading with data: Pathways to improve your school.* Thousand Oaks, CA: Corwin.

Gray, K. C. (1999). *Getting real: Helping teens find their future.* Thousand Oaks, CA: Corwin.

Halstead, J. M., & Pike, M. (2006). *Citizenship and moral education: Values in action.* New York: Routledge.

Harris, S. (2005). *Bravo teacher! Building relationships with actions that value others.* Larchmont, NY: Eye on Education.

Holcomb, E. L. (2001). *Asking the right questions: Techniques for collaboration and school change* (2nd ed.). Thousand Oaks, CA: Corwin.

Houston, P. D., & Sokolow, S. L. (2006). *The spiritual dimension of leadership: 8 key principles to leading more effectively.* Thousand Oaks, CA: Corwin.

Hoy, W. H., & Miskel, C. G. (1996). *Educational administration: Theory, research, and practice* (5th ed.). New York: McGraw-Hill

Hoyle, J. R. (2002). *Leadership and the force of love: Six keys to motivating with love.* Thousand Oaks, CA: Corwin.

Hoyle, J. (2006). *Leadership and futuring: Making visions happen* (2nd ed.). Thousand Oaks, CA: Corwin.

Israel, S. E., Sisk, D. A., & Block, C. C. (2006). *Collaborative literacy: Using gifted strategies to enrich learning for every student.* Thousand Oaks, CA: Corwin.

Jayanthi, M., & Nelson, J. S. (2001). *Savvy decision making: An administrator's guide to using focus groups in schools.* Thousand Oaks, CA: Corwin.

Johnson, S. (1998). *Who moved my cheese?* New York: Putnam.

Johnston, G. L., Townsend, R. S., Gross, G. E., Lynch, P., Garcy, L. M., Roberts, B. B., et al. (2009). *The superintendent's planner: A monthly guide and reflective journal.* Thousand Oaks, CA: Corwin.

Josephson, M. S., & Hanson, W. (1998). *The power of character.* San Francisco: Jossey-Bass.

Kaser, J., Mundry, S., Stiles, K. E., Loucks-Horsley, S. (2001). *Leading every day: 124 actions for effective leadership.* Thousand Oaks, CA: Corwin.

Kilmek, K. J., Ritzenhein, E., & Sullivan, K. D. (2008). *Generative leadership: Shaping new futures for today's schools.* Thousand Oaks, CA: Corwin.

Kochanek, J. R. (2005). *Building trust for better schools: Research-based practices.* Thousand Oaks, CA: Corwin.

Kosmoski, G. J., & Pollack, D. R. (2000). *Managing difficult, frustrating, and hostile conversations: Strategies for savvy administrators.* Thousand Oaks, CA: Corwin.

Kouzes, J. M., & Posner, B. Z. (1998). *Encouraging the heart: A leader's guide to rewarding and recognizing others.* San Francisco: Jossey-Bass.

Kowalski, T. J. (2006). *The school superintendent: Theory, practice, and cases.* Thousand Oaks, CA: Sage Publications.

Krovetz, M. L. (2008). *Fostering resilience: Expecting all students to use their minds and hearts well* (2nd ed.). Thousand Oaks, CA: Corwin.

Krzyzewski, M., & Phillips, D. T. (2000). *Leading with the heart: Coach K's successful strategies for basketball, business, and life.* New York: Warner Books.

Leithwood, K. (Ed.). (1995). *Effective school leadership: Transforming politics into education.* Thousand Oaks, CA: Corwin.

Longworth, N. (2006). *Learning cities, learning regions, learning communities: Lifelong learning and local government.* New York: Routledge.

Louis, K. S. (2005). *Organizing for school change.* New York: Routledge.

Lovely, S. (2006). *Setting leadership priorities: What's necessary, what's nice, and what's got to go.* Thousand Oaks, CA: Corwin.

Maxwell, J. C. (1995). *Developing the leaders around you.* Nashville, TN: Thomas Nelson.

McEwan, E. K. (1997). *Leading your team to excellence: How to make quality decisions.* Thousand Oaks, CA: Corwin.

McEwan, E. K. (1998). *How to deal with parents who are angry, troubled, afraid, or just plain crazy.* Thousand Oaks, CA: Corwin.

Miller, J. P. (2006). *Educating for wisdom and compassion: Creating conditions for timeless learning.* Thousand Oaks, CA: Corwin.

Olssen, M., Codd, J. A., & O'Neill, A. (2004). *Education policy: Globalization, citizenship and democracy.* Thousand Oaks, CA: Sage Publications.

Osier, J. L., & Fox, H. P. (2001). *Settle conflicts right now! A step-by-step guide for K–6 classrooms.* Thousand Oaks, CA: Corwin.

Osterman, K. F., & Kottkamp, R. B. (2004). *Reflective practice for educators: Professional development to improve student learning.* Thousand Oaks, CA: Corwin.

Palestini, R. H. (1999). *Educational administration: Leading with mind and heart.* Lancaster, PA: Technomic.

Pellicer, L. O. (1999). *Caring enough to lead: Schools and the sacred trust.* Thousand Oaks, CA: Corwin.

Pellicer, L. O. (2003). *Caring enough to lead: How reflective thought leads to moral leadership.* Thousand Oaks, CA: Corwin.

Peters, T., & Waterman, R. H. (1993). *In search of excellence.* New York: Warner Books.

Podesta, C. (1993). *Self-esteem and the 6-second secret* (updated ed.). Thousand Oaks, CA: Corwin.

Podesta, C., & Sanderson, V. (1999). *Life would be easy if it weren't for other people.* Thousand Oaks, CA: Corwin.

Pryor, B. W., & Pryor, C. R. (2005). *The school leader's guide to understanding attitude and influencing behavior: Working with teachers, parents, students, and the community.* Thousand Oaks, CA: Corwin.

Ralston, E. W., & MacKay, L. L. (1999). *Creating better schools.* Thousand Oaks, CA: Corwin.

Ramsey, R. D. (1999). *Lead, follow, or get out of the way.* Thousand Oaks, CA: Corwin.

Reagan, T. G., Case, C. W., & Brubacher, J. W. (2000). *Becoming a reflective educator: How to build a culture of inquiry in the schools.* Thousand Oaks, CA: Corwin.

Rebore, R. W., & Walmsley, A. L. E. (2009). *Genuine school leadership: Experience, reflection, and beliefs.* Thousand Oaks, CA: Corwin.

Reinhartz, J., & Beach, D. M. (2001). *Foundations of educational leadership: Changing schools, changing roles.* Boston: Allyn & Bacon.

Roberts, S. M., & Pruitt, E. Z. (2003). *Schools as professional learning communities: Collaborative activities and strategies for professional development.* Thousand Oaks, CA: Corwin.

Rubin, H. (2002). *Collaborative leadership: Developing effective partnerships in communities and schools* (2nd ed.). Thousand Oaks, CA: Corwin.

Sanders, M. G. (2006). *Building school-community partnerships: Collaboration for student success.* Thousand Oaks, CA: Corwin.

Schmieder, J. H., & Cairns, D. (1996). *Ten skills of highly effective principals.* Lancaster, PA: Technomic.

Schumaker, D. R., & Sommers, W. A. (2001). *Being a successful principal: Riding the wave of change without drowning.* Thousand Oaks, CA: Corwin.

Seiler, T. L. (2001). *Developing your case for support.* San Francisco: Jossey-Bass.

Sergiovanni, T. J. (1990). *Value-added leadership: How to get extraordinary performance in schools.* Orlando, FL: Harcourt Brace Jovanovich.

Sergiovanni, T. J. (1992). *Moral leadership: Getting to the heart of school improvement.* San Francisco: Jossey-Bass.

Sergiovanni, T. J. (1994). *Building community in schools.* San Francisco: Jossey-Bass.

Sergiovanni, T. J. (2001). *The principalship: A reflective practice perspective* (4th ed.). Needham Heights, MA: Allyn & Bacon.

Sergiovanni, T. J. (2007). *Rethinking leadership: A collection of articles* (2nd ed.). Thousand Oaks, CA: Corwin.

Sharp, W. L., Walter, J. K., & Sharp, H. M. (1998). *Case studies for school leaders: Implementing the ISLLC standards.* Lancaster, PA: Technomic.

Skrla, L., Erlandson, D. A., Reed, E. M., & Wilson, A. P. (2001). *The emerging principalship.* Larchmont, NY: Eye on Education.

Smith, M. L., Miller-Kahn, L., Heinecke, W., & Jarvis, P. F. (2003). *Political spectacle and the fate of American schools.* New York: Routledge.

Snowden, P. E., & Gorton, R. A. (1998). *School leadership and administration: Important concepts, case studies, and simulations* (5th ed.). New York: McGraw-Hill.

Sparks, D. (2006). *Leading for results: Transforming teaching, learning, and relationships in schools.* Thousand Oaks, CA: Corwin.

Spears, L., Lawrence, M., & Blanchard, K. (2002). *Focus on leadership: Servant-leadership for the 21st century.* New York: Wiley & Sons.

Sperry, D. J. (1999). *Working in a legal and regulatory environment: A handbook for school leaders.* Larchmont, NY: Eye on Education.

Streshly, W. A., Walsh, J., & Frase, L. E. (2001). *Avoiding legal hassles: What school administrators really need to know* (2nd ed.). Thousand Oaks, CA: Corwin.

Strike, K. A. (2007). *Ethical leadership in schools: Creating community in an environment of accountability.* Thousand Oaks, CA: Corwin.

Sullivan, S., & Glanz, J. (2006). *Building effective learning communities: Strategies for leadership, learning, & collaboration.* Thousand Oaks, CA: Corwin.

Taulbert, C. L. (2006). *Eight habits of the heart for educators: Building strong school communities through timeless values.* Thousand Oaks, CA: Corwin.

Terrell, R. D., & Lindsey, R. B. (2009). *Culturally proficient leadership: The personal journey begins within.* Thousand Oaks, CA: Corwin.

Thomas, S. J. (1999). *Designing surveys that work! A step-by-step guide.* Thousand Oaks, CA: Corwin.

Townsend, R. S., Johnston, G. L., Gross, G. E., Lynch, P., Roberts, B., Novotney, P. B., et al. (2006). *Effective superintendent-school board practices: Strategies for developing and maintaining a good relationship with your board.* Thousand Oaks, CA: Corwin.

Trump, K. S. (1998). *Practical school security: Basic guidelines for safe and secure schools.* Thousand Oaks, CA: Corwin.

Veale, J. R., Morley, R. E., & Erickson, C. L. (2001). *Practical evaluation for collaborative services: Goals, processes, tools, and reporting systems for school-based programs.* Thousand Oaks, CA: Corwin.

Wachter, J. C. (1999). *Classroom volunteers: Uh-oh! Or right on!* Thousand Oaks, CA: Corwin.

Weiss, H. B., Kreider, H., & Labez, M. E. (2005). *Preparing educators to involve families: From theory to practice.* Thousand Oaks, CA: Sage Publications.

West, C. E., & Derrington, M. L. (2009). *Leadership teaming: The superintendent-principal relationship.* Thousand Oaks, CA: Corwin.

Whitaker, T. A., Whitaker, B., & Lumpa, D. (2000). *Motivating and inspiring teachers: The educational leader's guide for building staff morale.* Larchmont, NY: Eye on Education.

Williams, R. B. (2006). *More than 50 ways to build team consensus.* Thousand Oaks, CA: Corwin.

Wilmore, E. L. (2008). *Superintendent leadership: Applying the educational leadership constituent council standards for improved district performance.* Thousand Oaks, CA: Corwin.

York-Barr, J., Sommers, W. A., Ghere, G. S., & Montie, J. (2006). *Reflective practice to improve schools: An action guide for educators.* Thousand Oaks, CA: Corwin.

DOMAIN 2

Banks, J. (2006). *Race, culture, and education: The selected works of James A. Banks.* New York: Routledge.

Banks, J. A., & Banks, C. M. (1996). *Multicultural education: Issues and perspectives.* Boston: Allyn & Bacon.

Barker, C. L., & Searchwell, C. J. (1998). *Writing meaningful teacher evaluations—right now!!* Thousand Oaks, CA: Corwin.

Barker, C. L., & Searchwell, C. J. (2001). *Writing year-end teacher improvement plans—right now!!* Thousand Oaks, CA: Corwin.

Barth, R. S. (2003). *Lessons learned: Shaping relationships and the culture of the workplace.* Thousand Oaks, CA: Corwin.

Beach, D. M., & Reinhartz, J. (2000). *Supervisory leadership.* Boston: Allyn & Bacon.

Beane, J. A. (1997). *Curriculum integration: Designing the core of democratic education.* New York: Teachers College Press.

BenShea, N. (2006). *The journey to greatness: And how to get there!* Thousand Oaks, CA: Corwin.

Bigge, M. L., & Shermis, S. S. (1999). *Learning theories for teachers* (6th ed.). New York: Addison-Wesley Longman.

Bjork, L. G., & Kowalski, T. J. (Eds.). (2005). *The contemporary superintendent: Preparation, practice, and development.* Thousand Oaks, CA: Corwin.

Blanchard, K., & Johnson, S. (1981). *The one minute manager.* New York: Berkley.

Blankenstein, A. M. (2004). *Failure is not an option: Six principles that guide student achievement in high-performing schools.* Thousand Oaks, CA: Corwin.

Blase, J., & Kirby, P. C. (1992). *Bringing out the best in teachers: What effective principals do.* Thousand Oaks, CA: Corwin.

Bocchino, R. (1999). *Emotional literacy: To be a different kind of smart.* Thousand Oaks, CA: Corwin.

Bolman, L., & Deal, T. (1995). *Path to school leadership.* Thousand Oaks, CA: Corwin.

Bracey, G. W. (2000). *Bail me out! Handling difficult data and tough questions about public schools.* Thousand Oaks, CA: Corwin.

Brewer, E. W., DeJonge, J. O., & Stout, V. J. (2001). *Moving online: Making the transition from traditional instruction and communication strategies.* Thousand Oaks, CA: Corwin.

Brooks-Young, S. (2007). *Critical technology issues for school leaders.* Thousand Oaks, CA: Corwin.

Bucher, R. D. (2000). *Diversity consciousness: Opening our minds to people, cultures, and opportunities.* Upper Saddle River, NJ: Prentice Hall.

Burrello, L. C., Lashley, C., & Beatty, E. E. (2001). *Educating all students together: How school leaders create unified systems.* Thousand Oaks, CA: Corwin.

Burton, V. R. (2000). *Rich minds, rich rewards.* Dallas, TX: Pearl.

Capper, C. A., & Frattura, E. M. (2009). *Meeting the needs of students of all abilities: How leaders go beyond inclusion* (2nd ed.). Thousand Oaks, CA: Corwin.

Carbo, M. (2000). *What every principal should know about teaching reading.* Syosset, NY: National Reading Styles Institute.

Carr, J. F., & Harris, D. (2009). *Improve standards-based learning: A process guide for educational leaders.* Thousand Oaks, CA: Corwin.

Cherry, D., & Spiegel, J. (2006). *Leadership, myth, & metaphor: Finding common ground to guide effective school change.* Thousand Oaks, CA: Corwin.

Costa, A. L., & Garmston, R. J. (1994). *Cognitive coaching.* Norwood, MA: Christopher Gordon.

Creighton, T. B. (2007). *Schools and data: The educator's guide for using data to improve decision making* (2nd ed.). Thousand Oaks, CA: Corwin.

Crow, G. M., & Matthews, L. J. (1998). *Finding one's way: How mentoring can lead to dynamic leadership.* Thousand Oaks, CA: Corwin.

Danielson, C., & McGreal, T. L. (2000). *Teacher evaluation to enhance professional practice.* Princeton, NJ: Educational Testing Service.

Daresh, J. (2001). *Leaders helping leaders: A practical guide to administrative mentoring* (2nd ed.). Thousand Oaks, CA: Corwin.

Daresh, J. C. (2002*). Teachers mentoring teachers: A practical approach to helping new and experienced staff.* Thousand Oaks, CA: Corwin.

Deal, T. E., & Peterson, K. D. (1994). *The leadership paradox.* San Francisco: Jossey-Bass.

Deal, T. E., & Peterson, K. D. (1999). *Shaping school culture: The heart of leadership.* San Francisco: Jossey-Bass.

Deli'Olio, J., & Donk, T. (2007). *Models of teaching: Connecting student learning with standards.* Thousand Oaks, CA: Sage Publications.

Denmark, V. M., & Podsen, I. J. (2000). *Coaching and mentoring first-year and student teachers.* Larchmont, NY: Eye on Education.

Earl, L. M., & Katz, S. (2006). *Leading schools in a data-rich world: Harnessing data for school improvement.* Thousand Oaks, CA: Corwin.

English, F. W. (2000). *Deciding what to teach and test: Developing, aligning, and auditing the curriculum.* Thousand Oaks, CA: Corwin.

Erickson, L. H. (2002). *Concept-based curriculum and instruction: Teaching beyond the facts.* Thousand Oaks, CA: Corwin.

Fichtman Dana, N., & Yendol-Hoppey, D. (2008). *The reflective educator's guide to professional development: Coaching inquiry-oriented learning communities.* Thousand Oaks, CA: Corwin.

Ford, B. A., & Obiakor, F. E. (2002). *Creating successful learning environments for African American learners with exceptionalities.* Thousand Oaks, CA: Corwin.

Glanz, J. (1998). *Action research: An educational guide to school improvement.* Norwood, MA: Christopher Gordon.

Glatthorn, A. A. (2001). *The principal as curriculum leader* (2nd ed.). Thousand Oaks, CA: Corwin.

Glatthorn, A. A., Boshcee, F., & Bruce, W. M. (2006). *Curriculum leadership: Development and implementation.* Thousand Oaks, CA: Sage Publications.

Glenn, H. S., & Brock, M. L. (1998). *7 strategies for developing capable students.* Roseville, CA: Prima.

Grady, M. L., & Brock, B. L. (2001). *From first-year to first-rate*: Principals guiding beginning teachers. Thousand Oaks, CA: Corwin.

Gregory, G. H., & Chapman, C. (2007). *Differentiated instructional strategies: One size doesn't fit all.* Thousand Oaks, CA: Corwin.

Guskey, T. R. (2000). *Evaluating professional development.* Thousand Oaks, CA: Corwin.

Hadaway, N., Vardell, S. M., & Young, T. (2001). *Literature-based instruction with English language learners.* Boston: Allyn & Bacon.

Holcomb, E. L. (1998). *Getting excited about data: How to combine people, passion, and proof.* Thousand Oaks, CA: Corwin.

Holt, L. C., & Kysika, M. (2006). *Instructional patterns: Strategies for maximizing student learning.* Thousand Oaks, CA: Sage Publications.

Hoyle, J. H., English, F., & Steffy, B. (1998). *Skills for successful 21st century school leaders.* Arlington, VA: American Association of School Administrators.

Irby, B. J., & Brown, G. (2000). *The career advancement portfolio.* Thousand Oaks, CA: Corwin.

Jarvis, P. (2007). *Lifelong learning and the learning society: Requirements and provision.* Florence, KY: Routledge.

Johnson, R. S. (2002). *Using data to close the achievement gap: How to measure equity in our schools.* Thousand Oaks, CA: Corwin.

Johnson, R. S., Mims-Cox, J. S., & Doyle-Nichols, A. (2006). *Developing portfolios in education: A guide to reflection, inquiry, and assessment.* Thousand Oaks, CA: Sage Publications.

Joyce, B., & Weil, M. (1996). *Models of teaching.* Needham Heights, MA: Simon & Schuster.

Joyner, E. T., Ben-Avie, M., & Comer, J. P. (2004). *Transforming school leadership and management to support student learning and development: The field guide to Comer schools in action.* Thousand Oaks, CA: Corwin.

Joyner, E. T., Comer, J. P., & Ben-Avie, M. (2004). *Comer schools in action: The 3-volume field guide.* Thousand Oaks, CA: Corwin.

Kennedy, E. (2003). *Raising test scores for all students: An administrator's guide to improving standardized test performance.* Thousand Oaks, CA: Corwin.

Kimmelman, P. L. (2006). *Implementing NCLB: Creating a knowledge framework to support school improvement.* Thousand Oaks, CA: Corwin.

Kozol, J. (1992). *Savage inequalities: Children in America's schools.* New York: Harper.

Kozol, J. (2000). *Ordinary resurrections: Children in the years of hope.* New York: Crown.

Leithwood, K., Aitken, R., & Jantzi, D. (2001). *Making schools smarter: A system for monitoring school and district progress* (2nd ed.). Thousand Oaks, CA: Corwin.

Love, N. (2009). *Using data to improve learning for all: A collaborative inquiry approach.* Thousand Oaks, CA: Corwin.

Maanum, J. L. (2009). *The general educator's guide to special education* (3rd ed.). Thousand Oaks, CA: Corwin.

Martin, L. C. (2009). *Strategies for teaching students with learning disabilities.* Thousand Oaks, CA: Corwin.

McCabe, N., Cunningham, L. L., Harvey, J., & Koff, R. H. (2005). *The superintendent's fieldbook: A guide for leaders of learning.* Thousand Oaks, CA: Corwin.

McTighe, J., & Arter, J. (2001). *Scoring rubrics in the classroom: Using performance criteria for assessing and improving student performance.* Thousand Oaks, CA: Corwin.

Metzger, C. (2006). *Balancing leadership and personal growth: The school administrator's guide.* Thousand Oaks, CA: Corwin.

Monahan, T. (2005). *Globalization, technological change, and public education.* New York: Routledge.

Montgomery, K., & Wiley, D. (2004). *Creating E-portfolios using PowerPoint: A guide for educators.* Thousand Oaks, CA: Sage Publications.

Moore, K. (2005). *Effective instructional strategies: From theory to practice.* Thousand Oaks, CA: Sage Publications.

Moxley, D. E., & Taylor, R. T. (2006). *Literacy coaching: A handbook for school leaders.* Thousand Oaks, CA: Corwin.

Nicholls, G. (2005). *The challenge to scholarship: Rethinking learning, teaching and research.* New York: RoutledgeFalmer.

Nicoll, K. (2006*). Flexibility and lifelong learning: Policy, discourse and politics.* New York: Routledge.

Nielsen, L. B. (2002). *Brief reference of student disabilities.* Thousand Oaks, CA: Corwin.

Oliva, P. F. (1997). *Supervision in today's schools* (5th ed.). New York: John Wiley.

Osborne, A. G., & Russo, C. J. (2009). *Discipline in special education.* Thousand Oaks, CA: Corwin.

Page, M. L., & Marlowe, B. A. (1998). *Creating and sustaining the constructivist classroom.* Thousand Oaks, CA: Corwin.

Payne, R. K. (1998). *A framework for understanding poverty.* Baytown, TX: RFT.

Peterson, K. D. (2002). *Effective teacher hiring: A guide to getting the best.* Alexandria, VA: Association for Supervision & Curriculum Development.

Podsen, I. J. (2002). *Teacher retention: What is your weakest link?* Larchmont, NY: Eye on Education.

Pratt, D. (1994). *Curriculum planning: A handbook for professionals.* Ft. Worth, TX: Harcourt Brace.

Reiss, K. (2006). *Leadership coaching for educators: Bringing out the best in school administrators.* Thousand Oaks, CA: Corwin.

Reksten, L. E. (2000). *Using technology to increase student learning.* Thousand Oaks, CA: Corwin.

Reksten, L. E. (2009). *Sustaining extraordinary student achievement.* Thousand Oaks, CA: Corwin.

Robinson, V., & Lai, M. K. (2006). *Practitioner research for educators: A guide to improving classrooms and schools.* Thousand Oaks, CA: Corwin.

Sagor, R. (2005). *The action research guidebook.* Thousand Oaks, CA: Corwin.

Schlechty, P. C. (2001). *Shaking up the school house.* San Francisco: Jossey-Bass.

Schmuck, R. (2006). *Practical action research for change* (2nd ed.). Thousand Oaks, CA: Corwin.

Sergiovanni, T. J. (1996). *Leadership for the schoolhouse: How is it different? Why is it important?* San Francisco: Jossey-Bass.

Sergiovanni, T. J. (2000). *The lifeworld of leadership: Creating culture, community, and personal meaning in our schools.* San Francisco: Jossey-Bass.

Sergiovanni, T. J., & Starratt, R. J. (1998). *Supervision: A redefinition* (6th ed.). Boston: McGraw-Hill.

Sharp, W. L., Walter, J. K., & Sharp, H. M. (1998). *Case studies for school leaders: Implementing the ISLLC standards.* Lancaster, PA: Technomic.

Showers, B., & Joyce, B. (2002). *Student achievement through staff development* (3rd ed.). Alexandria, VA: Association for Supervision & Curriculum Development.

Skrla, L., McKenzie, K. B., & Scheurich, J. J. (2009). *Using equity audits to create equitable and excellent schools.* Thousand Oaks, CA: Corwin.

Solomon, P. G. (2002). *The assessment bridge: Positive ways to link tests to learning, standards, and curriculum improvement.* Thousand Oaks, CA: Corwin.

Strickland, C. A., & Glass, K. T. (2009). *Staff development guide for the parallel curriculum.* Thousand Oaks, CA: Corwin.

Sunderman, G. L. (2008). *Holding NCLB accountable: Achieving accountability, equity, & school reform.* Thousand Oaks, CA: Corwin.

Sunderman, G. L., Kim, J. S., & Orfield, G. (2005). *NCLB meets school realities: Lessons from the field.* Thousand Oaks, CA: Corwin.

Thompson, S. J., Quenemoen, R. F., Thurlow, M. L., & Ysseldyke, J. E. (2001). *Alternate assessments for students with disabilities.* Thousand Oaks, CA: Corwin.

Thurlow, M. L., Elliott, J. L., & Ysseldyke, J. E. (1998). *Testing students with disabilities: Practical strategies for complying with district and state requirements.* Thousand Oaks, CA: Corwin.

Tileston, D. W., & Darling, S. K. (2009). *Teaching students of poverty and diverse culture.* Thousand Oaks, CA: Corwin.

Tomlinson, C. A. (1999). *The differentiated classroom: Responding to the needs of all learners.* Alexandria, VA: Association for Supervision & Curriculum Development.

Tomlinson, C. A. (2001). *How to differentiate instruction in mixed-ability classrooms* (2nd ed.). Alexandria, VA: Association for Supervision & Curriculum Development.

Tomlinson, C. A., & Allan, S. D. (2000). *Leadership for differentiating schools and classrooms.* Alexandria, VA: Association for Supervision & Curriculum Development.

Townsend, R. S., Johnston, G. L., Gross, G. E., Lynch, R., Garcy, L., Roberts, B., et al. (2007). *Effective superintendent-school board practices: Strategies for developing and maintaining good relationships with your board.* Thousand Oaks, CA: Corwin.

Walker, E., Sather, S. E., Norte, E., Katz, A., & Henze, R. C. (2002). *Leading for diversity: How school leaders promote interethnic relations.* Thousand Oaks, CA: Corwin.

Weil, J., Weil B., & Weil, M. (1998). *Models of teaching* (6th ed.). Needham Heights, MA: Simon & Schuster.

Whitaker, T. (1999). *Dealing with difficult teachers.* Larchmont, NY: Eye on Education.

Whitehead, B. M., Jensen, D. F. N., & Boschee, F. (2002). *Planning for technology: A guide for school administrators, technology coordinators, and curriculum leaders.* Thousand Oaks, CA: Corwin.

Williams, R. B. (2008). *Twelve roles of facilitators for school change* (2nd ed.). Thousand Oaks, CA: Corwin.

Wilmore, E. L. (2004). *Principal induction: A standards-based model for administrator development.* Thousand Oaks, CA: Corwin.

Wilmore, E. L. (2007). *Teacher leadership: Improving teaching and learning from inside the classroom.* Thousand Oaks, CA: Corwin.

Wolfe, P. (2001). *Brain matters: Translating research into classroom practice.* Alexandria, VA: Association for Supervision & Curriculum Development.

Woodward, J., & Cuban, L. (Eds.). (2001). *Technology, curriculum, and professional development: Adapting schools to meet the needs of students with disabilities.* Thousand Oaks, CA: Corwin.

Worthen, B., Sanders, J., & Fitzpatrick, J. (1996). *Program evaluation, alternative approaches and practical guidelines* (2nd ed.). New York: Addison-Wesley.

Ybarra, S., Hollingsworth, J., & Ardovino, J. (2000). *Multiple measures: Accurate ways to assess student achievement.* Thousand Oaks, CA: Corwin.

DOMAIN 3

Anderson, J. W. (2001). *The answers to questions that teachers most frequently ask.* Thousand Oaks, CA: Corwin.

Bennis, W. (1997). *Managing people is like herding cats.* Provo, UT: Executive Excellence.

Bjork, L. G., Kowalski, T. J. (2005). *The contemporary superintendent: Preparation, practice, and development.* Thousand Oaks, CA: Corwin.

Brewer, E. W., Achilles, C. M., Fuhriman, J. R., & Hollingsworth, C. (2001). *Finding funding: Grantwriting from start to finish, including project management and Internet use.* Thousand Oaks, CA: Corwin.

Brunner, J. M., & Lewis, D. K. (2009). *Safe & secure schools: 27 strategies for prevention and intervention.* Thousand Oaks, CA: Corwin.

Burrup, P. E., Brimpley, V., Jr., & Garfield, R. R. (1998). *Financing education in a climate of change* (7th ed.). Boston: Allyn & Bacon.

Bush, T., & Middlewood, D. (2005). *Leading and managing people in education.* Thousand Oaks, CA: Sage Publications.

Cambron-McCabe, N. (2005). *The superintendent's fieldbook.* Thousand Oaks, CA: Corwin.

Coleman, M., & Anderson, L. (2000). *Managing finance and resources in education.* Thousand Oaks, CA: Corwin.

Collinson, V., & Cook, T. F. (2006). *Organizational learning: Improving learning, teaching, and leading in school systems.* Thousand Oaks, CA: Sage Publications.

Covey, S. R. (1990). *The 7 habits of highly effective people.* New York: Simon & Schuster.

DiGiulio, R. C. (2001). *Educate, medicate, or litigate? What teachers, parents, and administrators must do about student behavior.* Thousand Oaks, CA: Corwin.

Dunklee, D. R., & Shoop, R. J. (2006). *The principal's quick-reference guide to school law: Reducing liability, litigation, and other potential legal tangles.* Thousand Oaks, CA: Corwin.

Erlandson, D. A., Stark, P. L., & Ward, S. M. (1996). *Organizational oversight: Planning and scheduling for effectiveness.* Larchmont, NY: Eye on Education.

Eller, J., & Carlson, H. C. (2009). *So now you're the superintendent!* Thousand Oaks, CA: Corwin.

Fitzwater, I. (1996). *Time management for school administrators.* Rockport, MA: Proactive.

Fullan, M. (2005). *Leadership sustainability: System thinkers in action.* Thousand Oaks, CA: Corwin.

Hoyle, J. R., Bjork, L. G., Collier, V., Glass, T. (2005). *The superintendent as CEO: Standards-based performance.* Thousand Oaks, Corwin.

Imber, M., & Van Geel, T. (2000). *Education law* (2nd ed.). Mahwah, NJ: Lawrence Erlbaum Associates.

Knowles, C. (2002). *The first time grantwriter's guide to success.* Thousand Oaks, CA: Corwin.

Ledeen, M. A. (1999). *Machiavelli on modern leadership.* New York: St. Martin's.

Levenson, S. (2006). *Big-time fundraising for today's schools.* Thousand Oaks, CA: Corwin.

Lunenburg, F. C., & Ornstein, A. C. (2000). *Educational administration: Concepts and practices* (3rd ed.). Belmont, CA: Wadsworth/Thomas Learning.

Marazza, L. L. (2003). *The five essentials of organizational excellence: Maximizing schoolwide student achievement and performance.* Thousand Oaks, CA: Corwin.

McNamara, J. F., Erlandson, D. A., & McNamara, M. (1999). *Measurement and evaluation: Strategies for school improvement.* Larchmont, NY: Eye on Education.

McNeal, B., & Oxholm, T. (2009). *A school district's journey to excellence: Lessons from business and education.* Thousand Oaks, CA: Corwin.

Odden, A., & Archibald, S. (2001). *Reallocating resources: How to boost student achievement without asking for more.* Thousand Oaks, CA: Corwin.

Odden, A., & Kelley, C. (2002). *Paying teachers for what they know and do: New and smarter compensation strategies to improve schools.* Thousand Oaks, CA: Corwin.

Parsons, B. A. (2001). *Evaluative inquiry: Using evaluation to promote student success.* Thousand Oaks, CA: Corwin.

Peterson, S. (2001). *The grantwriter's Internet companion: A resource for educators and others seeking grants and funding.* Thousand Oaks, CA: Corwin.

Ramsey, R. D. (2001). *Fiscal fitness for school administrators: How to stretch resources and do even more with less.* Thousand Oaks, CA: Corwin.

Sanders, J. R. (2000). *Evaluating school programs* (2nd ed.). Thousand Oaks, CA: Corwin.

Schroth, G., Berkeley, T. R., & Fishbaugh, M. S. (2003). *Ensuring safe school environments.* Mahwah, NJ: Lawrence Erlbaum Associates.

Sergiovanni, T. J. (2000). *The lifeworld of leadership.* San Francisco: Jossey-Bass.

Shoop, R. J., & Dunklee, D. R. (2006). *Anatomy of a lawsuit: What every education leader should know about legal actions.* Thousand Oaks, CA: Corwin.

Slavin, R. E., & Fashola, O. S. (1998). *Show me the evidence! Proven and promising programs for America's schools.* Thousand Oaks, CA: Corwin.

Smith, H. W. (1994). *The 10 natural laws of successful time and life management.* New York: Warner Books.

Sorenson, R. D., & Goldsmith, L. M. (2006). *The principal's guide to school budgeting.* Thousand Oaks, CA: Corwin.

Thomson, S. (Ed.). (1993). *Principals of our changing schools: Knowledge and skill base.* Alexandria, VA: National Policy Board for Educational Administration.

References

Covey, S. R. (1990). *The 7 habits of highly effective people.* New York: Simon & Schuster.

Texas Education Agency. (2006). *Texas Examinations of Educator Standards: Preparation manual: 064 Superintendent.* Austin, TX: Author. Retrieved September 17, 2009, from www.texes.ets.org/assets/pdf/testprep_manuals/064_superintendent_55069_web.pdf

Texas Education Agency. (2006). *Texas Examinations of Educator Standards: Preparation manual: 064 Superintendent: District profile packet.* Austin, TX: Author. Retrieved September 17, 2009, from www.texes.ets.org/assets/pdf/testprep_manuals/064_superintendent2.pdf

Wilmore, E. L. (2003). *Passing the principal TExES exam: Keys to certification and school leadership.* Thousand Oaks: Corwin.

Wilmore, E. L. (2007). *Teacher leadership: Improving teaching and learning from inside the classroom.* Thousand Oaks, CA: Corwin.

Index

CORWIN
A SAGE Company

The Corwin logo—a raven striding across an open book—represents the union of courage and learning. Corwin is committed to improving education for all learners by publishing books and other professional development resources for those serving the field of PreK–12 education. By providing practical, hands-on materials, Corwin continues to carry out the promise of its motto: **"Helping Educators Do Their Work Better."**